T0319004

Cambridge Elements ≡

Elements in Beckett Studies
edited by
Dirk Van Hulle
University of Oxford
Mark Nixon
University of Reading

POSTCOGNITIVIST BECKETT

Olga Beloborodova
University of Antwerp

CAMBRIDGE
UNIVERSITY PRESS

CAMBRIDGE
UNIVERSITY PRESS

University Printing House, Cambridge CB2 8BS, United Kingdom

One Liberty Plaza, 20th Floor, New York, NY 10006, USA

477 Williamstown Road, Port Melbourne, VIC 3207, Australia

314–321, 3rd Floor, Plot 3, Splendor Forum, Jasola District Centre,
New Delhi – 110025, India

79 Anson Road, #06–04/06, Singapore 079906

Cambridge University Press is part of the University of Cambridge.

It furthers the University's mission by disseminating knowledge in the pursuit of education, learning, and research at the highest international levels of excellence.

www.cambridge.org
Information on this title: www.cambridge.org/9781108708616
DOI: 10.1017/9781108771108

First published 2020

A catalogue record for this publication is available from the British Library.

ISBN 978-1-108-70861-6 Paperback
ISSN 2632-0746 (online)
ISSN 2632-0738 (print)

Postcognitivist Beckett

Elements in Beckett Studies

DOI: 10.1017/9781108771108
First published online: April 2020

Olga Beloborodova
University of Antwerp

Author for correspondence: Olga Beloborodova,
olga.beloborodova@uantwerpen.be

Abstract: The aim of this Element is to offer a reassessment of Beckett's alleged Cartesianism using the theoretical framework of extended cognition – a cluster of present-day philosophical theories that question the mind's brain-bound nature and see cognition primarily as a process of interaction between the human brain and the environment it operates in. The principal argument defended here is that despite the Cartesian bias introduced by early Beckett scholarship, Beckett's fictional minds are not isolated 'skullscapes'. Instead, they are grounded in interaction with their fictional storyworlds, however impoverished those may have become in the later part of his writing career.

Keywords: Beckett studies, extended cognition, postcognitivism, fictional minds, Cartesian dualism

ISBNs: 9781108708616 (PB), 9781108771108 (OC)
ISSNs: 2632-0746 (online), 2632-0738 (print)

Contents

Introduction

The aim of this study is to present a new perspective on Beckett's fictional minds. Its theoretical backbone is the recently developed postcognitivist paradigm of extended cognition: the idea that the mind does not reside exclusively in the head, but rather extends into the world in a continuous and constitutive way. In foregrounding the hybridity of cognitive processes and states, postcognitivism rejects traditional brain-bound mind models, which in turn derive from the Cartesian principle of mind/world dualism. The Cartesian dualist doctrine, which has dominated philosophy of mind and cognitive science since the inception of both disciplines, treats the mind as an isolated, hermetically sealed, computer-like container that turns on mental representations and operates entirely independently from the lived, phenomenal world it inhabits.

Beckett's engagement with Cartesian philosophy has been widely acknowledged in Beckett studies. Many first-generation Beckett scholars had interpreted Beckett's oeuvre through the prism of Descartes' dualist doctrine, and their views became firmly entrenched in the decades that followed. More recently, however, the Cartesian Beckett hypothesis has been losing ground, due in no small measure to archival research which has revealed numerous other philosophical sources of influence, as well as Beckett's relatively limited knowledge of Descartes' work.

Without disputing the immense value of early Beckett scholarship, the present study provides a contribution to post-Cartesian Beckett studies by analysing Beckett's extended fictional minds in his prose. The principal argument defended here is that despite the Cartesian bias introduced by the first generation of Beckett scholars, Beckett's fictional minds are not isolated 'skullscapes'.[1] Instead, more often than not they are grounded in the interaction with their fictional storyworlds, however impoverished those may have become in the later part of his writing career. The postcognitivist reassessment of Beckett's work aims at fostering a new approach to the Beckettian mind, away from the canonical critical focus on introspection and towards a hybrid model of cognition.

The present study has the following structure: in the Introduction, postcognitivist theories of extended cognition will be briefly elucidated and contrasted with Cartesian dualism. Section 1 will then trace the emergence of the Cartesian bias in early Beckett studies and its evolution in recent decades. What this

---

[1] Linda Ben-Zvi derived her canonical term from an equally famous Beckettian image: '[w]hether light or dark, small or spacious, all these enclosures are variations of the same skullscape first explored by the Unnamable: "the inside of my distant skull where I once wandered, now am fixed"' (1986, 4).

survey demonstrates is that, in many cases, early Beckett scholars had good reasons for foregrounding Cartesian elements in Beckett's texts; however, other influences were often overlooked and alternative interpretations were lacking. Section 2 engages in a dialogue with this Cartesian perspective by discussing Beckett's prose works in order to flesh out his extended fictional minds. For reasons of scope, drama does not feature in Section 2 (and features only marginally in Section 1), although a postcognitivist reading certainly applies to Beckett's plays just as much as it does to Beckett's prose.[2]

The idea of a close interaction between the human brain and the environment it operates in goes back a long way and rose to unprecedented prominence during the early modernist period. William James, for example, treated consciousness as a function rather than an entity,[3] and the emerging field of phenomenology placed the emphasis on subjective experience. However, the twentieth century also witnessed a paradigm shift *away* from the notion of experience, partially as a reaction to the proliferation of 'unscientific' psychologism and behaviourism. The birth of analytic philosophy at the turn of the century and its later transformation into cognitive science in the 1950s, with rudimentary yet rapidly developing computers, has led to a fixation on the representational and computational models for the human brain. Such models assume that sensorimotor and environmental factors merely *cause* cognitive processes to occur inside the brain; in no way do they participate in cognition properly so-called (Rowlands, 2010, 30). Fortunately, in recent decades it has become clear that the clinical abstraction that underlies brain-bound models of cognition does not bring us much closer to solving the mystery of the human mind. As a result, an alternative, postcognitivist paradigm has emerged both in philosophy and cognitive science – one that brings the environment and material objects back under the spotlight of scientific scrutiny.

Extended cognition – an umbrella term for postcognitivist models used interchangeably with active externalism, 4E cognition,[4] and distributed cognition – insists on a dynamic and constitutive interaction between the biological brain, the

---

[2] To take just one example, the short play *Play* (1964) is grounded in the constitutive interaction between the characters and the light beam that prompts and cuts their speeches by jumping from one face to another, thus regulating their cognitive activity. For details on extended cognition in Beckett's drama, see Beloborodova 2018.

[3] In his 1904 essay, provocatively titled 'Does Consciousness Exist?', James explains that he only denies the existence of consciousness as one of the poles in a dualist system: 'I mean only to deny that the word stands for an *entity*, but to insist most emphatically that it does stand for a *function*. There is, I mean, no aboriginal stuff or quality of being, contrasted with that of which material objects are made, out of which our thoughts are made; but there is a function in experience which thoughts perform, and for the performance of which this quality is being evoked' (1996, 1–2; emphasis added).

[4] 4E cognition stands for embodied, embedded, enacted, and extended cognition (the four main strands in postcognitivism).

rest of the body, and the environment. Departing from a simple question – 'Where does the mind stop and the rest of the world begin?' (Clark and Chalmers, 2010, 27) – the proponents of extended cognition attempt to deal a significant blow to the hegemony of the Cartesian mind that has reigned supreme for centuries in the Western world, and thus dispense with the ubiquitous principle of mind/world dualism it entails.

For the present study, two theories of extended cognition will be of relevance, one more radically anti-Cartesian than the other. The less radical one is the *extended mind thesis*: according to its founding fathers, Andy Clark and David Chalmers, the extended mind thesis straddles the internal human brain and external objects (both material and immaterial) in a so-called hybrid or extended cognitive system. The idea is that both elements – neural and extracranial – are equally important: '[T]he human organism is linked with an external entity in a two-way interaction, creating a coupled system that can be seen as a cognitive system in its own right. . . . If we remove the external component the system's behavioural competence will drop, just as it would if we removed part of its brain' (Clark and Chalmers, 2010, 29). The extended mind thesis underwrites the traditional assumption that cognition is essentially information processing, and the only way to process information is to turn it into some form of representation. What it disputes, however, is the necessarily intracranial *location* of representations, claiming that they can also be external and functionally similar to their internal counterparts.

We use coupled cognitive systems all the time in our everyday lives. Consider the ways we rely on our content-bearing devices, such as smartphones and computers, to offload our long-term memory. However, the extended mind thesis goes beyond purely mnemonic functions, and a good example here is creative writing. As Richard Menary notes, 'an act of writing is supported by neural enabling processes as well as manipulations of the bodily external environment. We create and manipulate words and sentences in conjunction with relevant bodily and neural functions' (Menary, 2007, 622). Marco Bernini also refers to authors of fiction as 'extended-mind workers' (2014), foregrounding material agency as a constitutive part of a hybrid cognitive system.

Unlike the extended mind thesis, *enactivism*, the more radical member of the postcognitivist family, categorically rejects the representational account of cognition and claims that cognitive processes take place during the intelligent agent's unmediated interaction with their surroundings. It draws on the theories of the French phenomenologist Maurice Merleau-Ponty, who emphasised the importance of the body for human cognition and saw 'our bodies both as physical structures and as lived, experiential structures' (Varela et al., 1991, xv). This is how Varela, Thompson, and Rosch formulate the challenge of their enactivist theory: 'In the enactive program, we explicitly call into question the assumption – prevalent throughout cognitive science – that cognition consists of the representation of a world that is independent of our cognitive and perceptual capacities by a cognitive system that exists independent of the world' (page xx). More recently, Di Paolo, Rohde, and De Jaegher (2010) developed a set of five elements that constitute an enactive cognitive system: namely, autonomy or self-generation, sense-making, emergence, embodiment, and experience. The key feature of such a system is that it is not only *shaped* by the world it interacts with, but it also plays a constitutive role in *shaping* that world every time the interaction takes place. In other words, enactivism goes beyond rejecting the concept of mental representations as the motor of cognitive activity: it questions the very idea of a stable, pre-given world out there that only needs to be discovered by an otherwise passive organism. The idea is that the organism's cognitive actions 'modify the environment and/or the relation of the organism to its environment, and hence modify in return the sensory input' (Stewart, 2010, 3).

Even this brief description of two major postcognitivist strands reveals important differences in the way they situate the cognising agent within its environment. While the extended mind thesis, with its foregrounding of external objects as parts of a hybrid cognitive system, still underwrites the representational mind model and implicitly acknowledges the existence of the internal/external divide, enactivism abandons both of these premises – in their eyes still Cartesian – and reconceptualises cognition as a perpetual feedback loop with no pre-given representational structures stored in the neural brain or elsewhere.

1 Survey of Beckett Criticism

This section seeks to explore the critical appraisal of Beckett's engagement with philosophy. The first part investigates the Cartesian bias in early Beckett criticism and its gradual undoing in more recent scholarship, focusing on the rigid mind/world (or subject/object) dualism advocated by Descartes himself as well as his followers, such as Arnold Geulincx. The second part introduces a number of alternative philosophical schools (such as early Greek philosophy, phenomenology, and extended cognition) that have been gaining increasing prominence as Beckett studies matured.

Ironically, Beckett studies have been plagued by all manner of dualisms from the very start: French-speaking vs Anglophone, modernist vs postmodernist, humanist vs poststructuralist, and so on. In this connection, the Cartesian bias in early Anglophone Beckett studies has been seen as a counterweight to the existentialist trend in Francophone Beckett scholarship (Morot-Sir, 1976, 29–30; Feldman and Madmami, 2015, 15). From the 1980s onwards, new fields of enquiry such as 'Beckett and the archive', 'Beckett in context', and 'Embodied Beckett' began to emerge, possibly as an alternative to the post-structuralist/postmodernist/psychoanalytical wave of criticism that had its hey-day in the closing decades of the twentieth century (Pattie, 2000, 152–80). Without making any judgements as to the quality of earlier and more recent Beckett criticism, this section will investigate how Cartesianism in Beckett studies has fared since the discipline's inception, and how it has been affected by the growing attention to the archive and new developments in (cognitive) philosophy.

Cartesianism in Early Anglophone Beckett Studies

The story begins with Ruby Cohn's now legendary special issue of *Perspective* (1959). Devoted entirely to Beckett, it was the first comprehensive critical survey in Beckett studies, and as such immediately set the tone for years to come. Not only did the issue place Beckett's oeuvre firmly within a philosophical framework, it also established a profound connection with Descartes' dualist doctrine (Pattie, 2000, 105). A telltale sign is the fact that two of the five articles comprising the issue have the word 'Cartesian' already in their titles. Both articles – 'The Cartesian Centaur' by Hugh Kenner and 'Beckett's *Murphy*: A Cartesian Novel' by Samuel Mintz – later became canonical in Beckett studies.

It was Hugh Kenner who introduced some of the most enduring Cartesian imagery to Beckett scholarship. In the first section of his highly influential *Samuel Beckett: A Critical Study*, aptly titled 'The Man in the Room', Kenner writes that 'Malone in bed bears curious analogies with Descartes, whose speculations, notoriously detached from the immediate inspection of visible and audible things, were by preference pursued in the same place' (1961, 17).[5] Kenner also mentions Beckett's own 'siege in the room', from 1945 to 1950, which famously delivered *Waiting for Godot* and the Trilogy, preceded by an 'apprenticeship or Cartesian preparation' that consisted of Beckett '[spending] most of his days in bed' (21). This way, the connection between Malone, Beckett, and Descartes becomes almost biographical. The trope of the room, or any enclosed space, also receives a Cartesian explanation in Ruby Cohn's

---

[5] Morot-Sir draws a similar parallel (between Descartes and all Beckettian characters) in discussing the opposition between the road and the room, 'an opposition that is permanent in Beckett's work' (1976, 64). He associates the room with Descartes, and the road with Belacqua, and believes that 'Beckett's vision of humanity is dominated by those two couples', with the room being the 'center of perspective', the road 'the bridge', and 'all Beckettian events [deriving] from them' (65).

discussion of the four novellas: invoking the figure of Descartes as sketched in *Whoroscope*, she connects the loss of housing by the characters in 'L'Expulsé' and 'La Fin' to 'the Cartesian mind-body cleavage evict[ing] man from the dwelling in which he was formerly housed' (1962, 102). Besides, the protagonist of 'Le Calmant', just like Malone, 'wonders whether his room *is* a head, though not necessarily his own' (116–17).

Kenner detects Cartesian overtones in both Beckett's early and later writing: '[The Belacqua stories] turn on a discrepancy between the mind's operations and what the world presents' (1961, 41), whereas the later works all but dispense with the world. In Molloy's case, 'the phenomena of the visible world simply do not interest him. He tired of them, he gives us to understand, long ago' (60). As for the body, 'the late novels turn their surfaces . . . from the light, which falls on bodies in repetitious, cyclic, violent motion. (This is all that an orthodox Cartesian is likely to make of bodily activities, and Beckett from the first has found some variety of Cartesianism much to his taste)' (61). The physical is associated with the senseless, as is cruelty, and – once again – biographical facts are used as illustrations, as Kenner refers to Beckett's stabbing in Paris and the occupation of France during World War II.

In arguably his most famous contribution to the Cartesian debate in early Beckett studies, Kenner coined the term 'Cartesian Centaur' and turned the bicycle, a frequently encountered object in Beckett's novels, into a symbol of the mind–machine symbiosis. In the case of Molloy,

> man and machine *mingle* in *conjoint* stasis, each indispensable to the other's support. At rest, the bicycle *extends* and stabilizes Molloy's endoskeleton. In motion, it *complements* and *amends* his structural deficiencies . . . This odd machine exactly *complements* Molloy. It even compensates for his inability to sit down . . . and it transfers to an ideal, Newtonian plane . . . those locomotive expedients improbably complex for the intact human being, and for the crippled Molloy impossible. (1961, 118; emphasis added)

It is striking how this image, if read from a postcognitivist point of view, serves as a powerful illustration of the smooth interaction between the human subject and the inanimate object. Yet, for Kenner, '[t]his [Cartesian Centaur] rises clear of the muddle in which Descartes leaves the mind-body relationship. The intelligence guides, the mobile wonder obeys, and there is no mysterious interpenetration of function' (121). Kenner also quotes from 'The Calmative' to further illustrate his point: 'Down a dead street . . . passes at an unassignable time a phantom cyclist, all the while reading a paper which with two hands he holds unfolded before his eyes. So body and mind go each one nobly about its business, without interference or interaction' (121).

As is clear from the above examples, the main contradiction in Kenner's argument concerns the mind/body interaction. On the one hand, Kenner speaks of conjoining, extension, and complementation; he notes that the disintegration of Molloy, as well as of the Mercier–Camier tandem, begins with the demise of their bicycles (1961, 117, 128). On the other hand, he claims to see no communication between the two poles in the Cartesian dualist system, as the example of the phantom cyclist has shown.

Kenner's view on the Trilogy as a whole is equally Cartesian, as he sketches the following evolution of Descartes' doctrine across the three novels:

> *The Unnamable* is the final phase of a trilogy which carries the Cartesian process backwards, beginning with a bodily *je suis* and ending with a bare *cogito*. This reduction begins with a journey (Molloy's) and a dismemberment of the Cartesian Centaur; its middle term (*Malone Dies*) is a stasis, dominated by the unallayable brain; and the third phase has neither the identity of rest nor that of motion, functions under the sign neither of matter nor of mind because it evades both, and concerns itself endlessly to no end with a baffling intimacy between discourse and non-existence. (1961, 128–9)

He also finds support for his argument in stylistic features that Descartes' writing seems to share with the Trilogy. In particular, he quotes the following passage from Descartes: 'But there is nothing which that nature teaches me more expressly than that I have a body which is ill affected when I feel pain, and stands in need of food and drink when I experience the sensations of hunger and thirst, etc. And therefore I ought not to doubt but that there is some truth in these informations' (from *Meditation* VI, qtd in Kenner, 1961, 119). For Kenner,

> [the] last sentence, despite Descartes' proclaimed certainty, has Molloy's tone, and the whole passage … prompts comparison with certain speculations of The Unnamable: '… Equate me, without pity or scruple, with him who exists, somehow, no matter how, no finicking, with him who whose story this story had the brief ambition to be. Better, ascribe me to a body. Better still, arrogate me to a mind. Speak of a world of my own, sometimes referred to as the inner, without choking. Doubt no more. Seek no more.' (1961, 119–20)

One would indeed be hard-pressed to ignore the uncanny similarity Kenner is alluding to, which partially explains why early Beckett criticism was so keen on discovering Cartesian elements in Beckett's work: those elements *are* undoubtedly present both on and under the surface of Beckett's texts. Moreover, 'these fiats and revulsions come closer to the Cartesian spirit than Descartes himself' (Kenner, 1961, 120), because Beckett's protagonists completely lack the philosopher's unshakeable faith in God's good intentions: whereas Descartes states that 'God is no deceiver', the Unnamable 'assumes that the superior powers deceive continually' (120). This is why, in the words of Ruby Cohn, '[in Beckett's work] doubt does not, as in the *Cogito*, lead to a certainty of existence; doubt leads to more profound doubt' (1962, 102).

Unlike Kenner, who considers Cartesianism in Beckett's oeuvre across the board, Samuel Mintz focuses principally on *Murphy*. Pleading from the very start against 'the neatness of identifications', Mintz stresses that 'Beckett used Cartesianism . . . to give his novel structure, action, and meaning and not merely to exercise his intellectual ingenuity' (1959, 156). At the same time, he contends that *Murphy* is 'inexplicable' without reference to the Cartesian system that underlies the novel, namely that of Arnold Geulincx (156).[6] Mintz also flatly rejects the idea that Buddhist mysticism might be behind the third (dark) zone of Murphy's mind, since 'its roots go back no further than the dualism of Descartes and his followers' (157). Also, Murphy's belief both in 'the physical fact' and 'the mental fact' being 'equally real' suffices for Mintz to label him without further ado 'an orthodox Cartesian' (157).

It is interesting how Mintz, while remarking on 'Murphy's desire to isolate his mind or self from the world outside' (1959, 159), invokes the rocking chair as 'best suited' for the purpose without commenting on the fact that the chair itself is part of the material outside world Murphy tries to escape. Despite Murphy's earnest endeavours to leave 'the big blooming buzzing confusion' forever behind him, the world keeps bursting in, in the form of Celia, ginger biscuits, and the city of London – the latter enveloping Murphy on his numerous walks, and ultimately serving as his last resting place. Similarly, the Magdalen Mental Mercyseat, although seen by Murphy as a sanctuary, is still a replica of the big world, and the monad of Mr Endon's cell a mere 'representation', be it 'creditable', of the little world (160).

Besides invoking the Geulingian dualist system for *Murphy*, Mintz equates the protagonist's mind with Descartes' ('For Descartes's mind, read Murphy's mind', 1959, 161) and notes their common love for a warm environment. According to Bertrand Russell, 'Descartes's mind only worked when he was warm' (qtd in Mintz, 1959, 161), and Murphy relished his 'heated garret'. Ironically, reacting to an outside temperature is a bodily function, which rather undercuts Murphy's (and Descartes') radical mind/body split. It seems that the path to a life in the mind (whatever that may mean) will inevitably lie in both the body and the environment, as *Murphy*'s text continuously reminds us.

---

[6] In many ways, the dualism invoked by Geulincx is much more extreme than that preached by the great master himself: known as Occasionalism, Geulincx' doctrine denied any connection between the mind and the body (thus rejecting Descartes' pineal gland solution) and claimed that every physical and mechanical act is literally occasioned by God.

The way Mintz invokes the person (rather than the philosophy) of Descartes in his discourse could be a consequence of the excessive attention that early English-language Beckett studies paid to Beckett's poem *Whoroscope* (1930), which is more biographical than philosophical. Both Kenner and Cohn (among others) seem to attach a little too much weight to what could be considered an exercise in wit by a brilliant young writer eager to demonstrate his skill. Kenner sees in the Belacqua stories the Cartesian 'discrepancy between the mind's operations and what the world presents' (1961, 41), and in the same breath he links this to Descartes being the protagonist of *Whoroscope*. Similarly, John Fletcher states that '"Whoroscope" illustrates Beckett's lifelong fascination with Descartes' (1964, 27, also in Esslin, 1965, 25)[7] – an assertion that should raise a few eyebrows, considering that the poem was written at the beginning of Beckett's creative career at the tender age of twenty-four.[8] Ruby Cohn mentions, almost in passing, that Beckett 'received a Master's degree from Trinity in 1931, having done research on Descartes' (1962, 10). Although she does not go into detail as to what exactly Beckett researched, it has been assumed from the very beginning that Beckett's knowledge of the great Frenchman's work was comprehensive and thorough, and this has fuelled numerous Cartesian allusions that Beckett's work allegedly harbours.[9] As to the poem itself, what Cohn deems 'overwhelming erudition' (11) can also be interpreted as a youthful attempt to dazzle the world with knowledge that is as impressive as it is irrelevant (such as the way Descartes liked his eggs, for example). Cohn enumerates several characteristics described in the poem that Descartes apparently has in common with other Beckettian protagonists:

> Descartes's taste for a 'hot-cupboard' will be shared by Murphy; his love for a 'squinty doaty' by the hero of 'Premier Amour'. Beckett and his French heroes are as 'unmatinal' as Descartes himself.[10] Other Cartesian interests are

---

[7] In his article 'Beckett and the Cartesian Soul', Roger Scruton mentions Beckett's 'life-long *obsession* with Descartes' (1983, 230; emphasis added). Scruton also discusses 'certain philosophical theories that Beckett himself endorses here and there in his monograph on Proust ... The first, it almost goes without saying, is the Cartesian theory of mind' (230).

[8] At the same time, Fletcher admits that the poem 'came into being by chance' and had to be delivered very quickly: '[Beckett] had been reading Adrien Baillet's life of Descartes ... and so quite naturally used the material from it for his poem, written in a great hurry' (1964, 26). This hypothesis seems much more realistic than the one commonly advanced in early Beckett studies.

[9] According to Scruton, 'Beckett began his literary career with a thesis (never completed) on Descartes' (1983, 230). By contrast, Morot-Sir has the following to say on the subject: 'It seems that Beckett's research on Descartes had no relation with any formal academic obligation. Mr. Jerome Lindon, whom I consulted on this matter, very kindly replied that for *Whoroscope* Beckett utilized notes taken in the course of his studies in Dublin, but that he never wrote any school paper on the topic' (1976, 46–7).

[10] Similarly, Kenner talks about 'three attributes [that the Descartes of *Whoroscope*] shares with the protagonists of the future trilogy: a recurrent obsession (here, about eggs); an incapacity for

wheelchairs (*Endgame*), spectacles ('La Fin', *Waiting for Godot*, and *Endgame*), and slaughterhouses (almost all Beckett's French fiction). The early French heroes of Beckett imitate the Descartes of *Le Discours de la méthode*: 'I did nothing but roam from one place to another, desirous of being a spectator rather than an actor in the plays exhibited on the theatre of the world'. And all Beckett's work is an extrapolation of the Cartesian definition of man as 'a thing that thinks', so that knowledge begins with consciousness. (1962, 12–13)

The above quote demonstrates how easily (almost seamlessly) a transition is made from the person of Descartes – the protagonist of the early *Whoroscope* – to his philosophy, encompassing all of Beckett's work and reducing it to an expression of Cartesianism.[11]

Three years later, Ruby Cohn returns to the common features between Descartes' person and Beckett's characters (1965, 169–70), but this time she makes an important change in her formulation regarding the great Frenchman's philosophy in Beckett's work: 'Far more telling, however, than these incidental reminiscences is the fact that all Beckett's work paradoxically insists upon and rebels against the Cartesian definition of man as "a thing that thinks," insists upon and rebels against the knowledge that is confined within consciousness' (170). This qualification of her earlier statement reflects on Beckett's far from straightforward aesthetic treatment of Cartesian ideas. Commenting on Geulincx' variations on the dualist theme, Cohn characterises Murphy as 'a would-be Geulincxian' (1965, 170),[12] who 'seeks to withdraw from the physical world at large, and retire into his mind' (1962, 49), and suggests that 'subsequent Beckett heroes will, like Murphy, find themselves reluctant to accept the absolute Cartesian cleavage between body and mind: instead, they too will be attracted to Arnold Geulincx, the seventeenth-century Cartesian, who emphasized the delights of the mind' (49). However, 'the material world, the macrocosm, impinges upon Murphy; burned to death in his heated garret, Murphy loses mind along with body' (1965, 170). Here, Cohn seems to acknowledge Murphy's inability to sever the connection between his mind and his body and his failure to withdraw from the big world, which may point to a fundamental unity of mind, body, and the world they operate in.

Having said that, it is easy to see why Beckett's texts provide so much ammunition to plead the Cartesian case, particularly as far as mind/world dualism is concerned, even if its influence and particularly Beckett's knowledge

---

brushing the wing of his mind against persons or things without nausea; and a singular absence of what can only be called identity' (1961, 41).

[11] In his study of Beckett's 'Philosophy Notes', Matthew Feldman also holds *Whoroscope* partly responsible for the Cartesian bias of early Beckett studies (2006, 40–1).

[12] Although she also labels him (just like Watt) 'a latter-day Cartesian' (1965, 174).

of the subject matter may have been exaggerated in early Beckett studies. For an example of the mind/body dichotomy in Beckett's characters, Cohn invokes *Mercier and Camier*, where 'Mercier may be taken as a representative of the mind, and Camier of the body' (1965, 170).[13] She also traces the word 'conarium' to Camier's name by invoking 'the Irish meaning of the prefix "cam," somewhat analogous to the French "con," since the *conarium*, where Descartes thought mind joined body, is a favourite butt of Beckett's wit' (1962, 97), and refers to the episode in which 'a M. Conaire seeks Camier [the more "physical" of the two]. Descartes's *conarium*, where matter meets mind, is again relevant. Murphy was charged by Neary with a conarium, "shrunk to nothing". So, Camier, by rejecting M. Conaire's company, may be performing a symbolic "conarectomy", removing any possible meeting ground for mind and body' (1962, 98).

Clearly, there is ample textual evidence of Cartesian overtones in *Mercier and Camier*, and the same applies to the Trilogy. Just like Kenner, Cohn expounds on stylistic and substantive similarities between Beckett's texts and Descartes' discourse. For instance, when she describes the Unnamable 'as nearly a pure mentality as has appeared in fiction' (1962, 117), she finds 'a sentence in Book IV of *Le Discours de la méthode* [that] seems to foreshadow the Unnamable: "I could suppose that I had no body, and that there was no world nor any place in which I might be"' (117). Cohn also contends that the Unnamable's monologue is

> a virtual Discourse on Lack of Method, on the impossibility of method ... Like Descartes, the Unnamable subjects everything to doubt, but he never arrives at the certainty of a doubting subject. Like Descartes, the Unnamable postulates a malevolent divinity. Descartes' 'But there is I know not what being, who is possessed at once of the highest power and the deepest cunning, who is constantly employing all his ingenuity in deceiving me' (*Meditation* II), becomes the Unnamable's 'The essential is to go on squirming forever at the end of the line, as long as there are waters and banks and ravening in heaven a sporting God to plague his creatures'. (1965, 172–3)

Continuing to restate the Trilogy's mind/body opposition in a manner that exemplifies early Beckett scholarship, Cohn enumerates the gradual bodily degradation that Molloy and Moran undergo, followed by Malone's immobility

---

[13] A fellow 'Cartesian', John Fletcher disputes such a neat dichotomy in his comment on Cohn's analysis: 'Camier may be seen to represent the physical side in that he is, for instance, usually the more concerned with food, but at the same time he is the bachelor whereas Mercier is married with children, and it is the latter who describes himself as the wreck and his friend the tugboat, not the other way about' (1964, 116). Fletcher thus sees their tandem not as 'the enforced union of body and mind', but rather an attempt 'to avoid the horrors of solitude' (116). The same applies, in Fletcher's view, to the union between Vladimir and Estragon (116).

and the Unnamable's 'headless thought, mouthless speech, and earless listening to words that may or may not be his' (171). Unfortunately, she makes no connection between the characters' advanced bodily decay and their states of mind, such as Moran's growing confusion and the Unnamable's incoherent ravings at the end of the novel, which leaves the impression that while the body falls apart, the mind undergoes no change, further strengthening the idea of their separate existence.

John Fletcher, another monument of early Beckett studies, refers to the 'idea of a world within a skull' that 'recurs in *Murphy, Malone Dies* and *The Unnamable,* and so obsessive it is, evidently, that we find in *Cascando* ... the refrain "They say, It's in his head"' (1964, 29).[14] Fletcher's account of Beckett's novels (1964) is also pervaded with Cartesian allusions, although he does note Murphy's disappointing experience in the Magdalen Mental Mercyseat, where the supposedly 'self-immersed' patients 'are not as blissfully happy as he imagines' (52), and where he fails 'to clinch the issue in favour of the serenity of the mind for once and for all' (52). Moreover, '[t]he realization that he is a mere "speck in Mr. Endon's unseen" determines Murphy to abandon the Mercyseat and perhaps return to Celia' (52–3), which could signify a flight from the pure mind back to the body. Also, Fletcher perceptively remarks that Murphy fails to attain his mental bliss because 'even if it is possible to come alive in one's mind, it is not possible this side of the Styx to cut oneself off completely from the body' (53), and concludes that 'the fact that [Murphy] feels profoundly divided is ultimately the cause of the catastrophe that kills him' (53). Although the Cartesian dualist split (not just between Murphy's mind and his body, but also between Murphy's mind and the society in which he is expected to function) underlies Fletcher's account throughout, he does recognise that both the body and the world hold Murphy firmly in their grasp, and that his desperate attempts to escape into the 'closed system' of his mind are 'doomed to fail' and eventually lead to his demise.

Fletcher's discussion of *Molloy* continues to explore Cartesian themes, as the novel 'also takes up again the issue of dualism' (140). In *Molloy*, 'the body and mind are once more firmly separated', and '[t]he brain ... is by far the most reliable part of the body' (140). As an important nuance, Fletcher adds that 'the brain, as Descartes pointed out, is not synonymous with the mind, which in Beckett's work ever since Belacqua has been yearning ... for the reprieve of "ceasing to be an annex of the restless body", and ever since Murphy functions "not as an instrument but as a place"' (140–1). The spatial representation of the mind is nicely illustrated when Molloy speaks of his 'ruins', 'a place with neither plan nor bounds', 'a place

---

[14] What Fletcher fails to mention is that in that same play, the Opener vehemently denies 'it' being in his head by stating instead that there is nothing is his head (Beckett 1986, 300).

devoid of mystery', to which he goes 'perhaps more gladly there than anywhere else', a place 'where you find yourself, sometimes, not knowing how, and which you cannot leave at will' (Beckett, 2009b, 38, also qtd in Fletcher, 1964, 141). Spatial metaphors are also used to characterise Moran's 'wandering in his mind' and 'noting every detail of the labyrinth, its paths as familiar as those of [his] garden and yet ever new' (Beckett, 2009b, 110, also qtd in Fletcher, 1964, 141). Fletcher quotes Moran referring to his mind as a place 'where all I need is to be found' (141), and concludes that

> [s]uch a mind, self-sufficient, is quite detached from its accompanying body. Molloy sees his hand on his knee as an indistinguishable part of the external physical world, a foreign object 'which my knee felt tremble and of which my eyes saw the wrist only, the heavily veined back, the pallid row of knuckles'; and like a truly Cartesian machine, the body only works when instructions are sent from the brain: 'my feet ... never took me to my mother unless they received a definite order to do so'. (1964, 141–2)

Like Cohn, Fletcher remarks on 'the extraordinary contrast . . . between a body in full decay and a mind ratiocinating on, as agile as ever it was' (142) – a far from unequivocal assertion, considering Molloy's aforementioned reference to his mind as his 'ruins', Moran's mental unravelling at the end of his quest, or Watt's progressively inverted speech, not to mention the Unnamable's confused stream of words towards the end of his story. Furthermore, Fletcher points to the Beckettian hero's isolation 'from the world of sensibilia, immured in himself, sealed off' (142–3): 'ensconced . . . within the castle of his mind, the Beckettian hero is with difficulty made aware of events around him' (143).

Though he continues to toe the line of Cartesian dualism, Fletcher does acknowledge other formative philosophical influences, albeit with some disdain: '[a]lthough Beckett has at one time or another been attracted to the Presocratics, there is nothing to suggest that his interest has ever gone beyond the anecdotal and superficial' (1964, 122). Also, the early Greek doctrine and its representatives are said to be regularly parodied in Beckett's work, or at least used to 'suit his own artistic purposes' (124), while 'Vico was obviously a purely intellectual and passing interest' (126). This contrasts sharply with the presentation of Beckett's attitude to Descartes, 'whose life and thought have dominated Beckett's work from the beginning' (126). Like Cohn and Kenner, Fletcher enumerates ostensibly common features between Descartes and Beckett's person and characters:

> We may wonder why Descartes' life[15] held such fascination for Beckett. Many things may have attracted him: Descartes' *grasses matinées* so like those Beckett himself indulged in when he could; his quietism and

---

[15] Note the emphasis on 'life' rather than 'doctrine'.

unwillingness to be burned for views that he none the less held so faithfully, if discreetly; his dislike of wide reading, so like Murphy's . . . and his preference for exile and dislike of a fixed existence. Whatever the reasons, Beckett not only admired this thinker's life but read deeply in his philosophy, and traces of Descartes' influence can be found, as critics have not been slow to notice, in nearly all his writings. (129)

It is remarkable how the initially tentative, subjunctive tone in the beginning of the quote (with two uses of 'may') meanders into a regular, indicative mood at the end, even though no evidence is presented to support the argument. Reiterating what has by then become the critical mantra, Fletcher claims that '"Descartes' myth",[16] . . . it is no exaggeration to say, underlies the whole of Beckett's work' (130) and discusses the familiar dictum of failing bodies and unfailing minds of Beckettian characters, which he calls 'Cartesian men':

> [T]o replace the broken-down machine that they acquired somehow at birth, they seize on such non-fleshly aides as crutches, poles (Malone), or bicycles (Mercier and Camier, Molloy), which, as often as not, abandon them.[17] But these mishaps never prevent their minds from marching on as agile as ever – which clearly reveals their Cartesianism. In Beckettian as in Cartesian man, the body is utterly distinct from the mind and the mind is free to ignore the body's mishaps with the serenity of one who knows that they occur as it were on another planet. (130–1)

Indicative, too, is Fletcher's remark that Descartes' name is 'often mentioned' in Beckett's oeuvre, while the examples he provides – *Dream*, *More Pricks Than Kicks*, *Murphy*, *Proust* – all date from the early period of Beckett's writing career and, as such, hardly serve as proof of Descartes' lasting influence on Beckett's work.

Although there is convincing textual support for his argument, Fletcher's Cartesian bias manifests itself when he categorically asserts that 'all Beckett's heroes live firmly immured in their minds, all "seedy solipsists" like Murphy' (1964, 134). As a consequence, he tends to minimise some other philosophical influences (such as Democritus' atomism) and excludes others, most notably Schopenhauer, who is not even mentioned in his analysis. With regard to the latter, Fletcher is not alone: it is remarkable how Schopenhauer's influence has consistently been ignored beyond *Proust* by early Beckett scholarship, especially since the archive has revealed a wealth of material that points to the German

---

[16] Here, Fletcher is referring to Gilbert Ryle's *The Concept of Mind* (1949), a highly influential and just as highly contested philosophical work that vehemently rejects Cartesian dualism and advocates the principle of cognitive extension long before postcognitivism saw the light of day.

[17] This is another instance when the introduction of external objects is being emphasised, without, however, expounding on the role they play in shaping the characters' minds.

philosopher's substantial impact on Beckett's aesthetics. As Van Hulle and Nixon note, 'Arthur Schopenhauer is without a doubt one of the philosophers with whom Beckett had most affinity' (2013, 143). Their examination of Beckett's personal library has revealed traces of a detailed study of Schopenhauer's texts, and Beckett's letters to MacGreevy confirm his admiration for the great German thinker, particularly regarding the aesthetic side of his work.[18] For Fletcher, however, the Cartesian dogma is carved in stone: '[w]hatever the truth of the matter, one thing is certain. Beckett has ranged freely among the writings of many philosophers, where he has found confirmation and justification of *the metaphysical obsessions* that haunt his work: *the gulf set between body and mind,* and epistemological incertitude' (1964, 137; emphasis added).

Much more nuanced is David Hesla's landmark account of Beckett's oeuvre from a philosophical perspective, aptly titled *The Shape of Chaos* (1971), which 'does not leave Beckett an isolated prisoner in the Cartesian stocks' (Morot-Sir, 1976, 41). That said, Hesla does launch his enquiry at the Cartesian juncture, namely by briefly pausing at *Whoroscope*. He considers it 'extraordinarily appropriate that *Whoroscope* should be one of the first things Beckett published; for in retrospect we can see that Descartes' bifurcation of substance into mind and matter – unextended thinking substance and extended, unthinking substance – is one of the fundamental polarities that pervades all of the poet's work' (16). Like Kenner (1961, 124–5), Hesla refers to Descartes' idea of 'the human body as an automaton', and he also notes that Beckett's representation of the body is a far cry from the perfectly attuned machine 'made by the hands of God' that Descartes so admired (16). As Kenner ironically remarks, 'unlike that of Molloy, the Cartesian body seems not subject to loss of toes or arthritis of the wrists' (1961, 120). Another example of the body as an 'automaton' comes from *How It Is*: 'ten yards fifteen yards semi-side left right leg right arm push pull flat on face imprecations no sound semi-side right left leg left arm push pull flat on face imprecations no sound not an iota to be changed in this description' (qtd in Hesla, 1971, 16). The repetitive, mechanistic and rhythmical texture of the passage certainly reinforces Hesla's Cartesian automaton interpretation, but Descartes' and Beckett's ideas on the mind's control over the body diverge radically on one point: 'believing as he did in the integrating function of the conarium, [Descartes] thought mind and matter worked together in sweetest harmony. In Beckett's view, however, they are joined in mortal combat' (17).

It is clear from the above overview that early Beckett scholarship's Cartesian bias was not always ill-founded, although the importance attached to *Whoroscope* does seem a little overstated. Especially with regard to early

---

[18] For a book-length study of Schopenhauer in Beckett's work, see Pothast 2008.

works, it is difficult not to spot Cartesian overtones and (often blatant) dualist oppositions. However, the way Descartes' philosophy and person were foregrounded at the expense of other possible influences is striking. Needless to say, the above overview does not pretend to be either exhaustive or comprehensive; at the same time, it can be considered representative of the state of the art in early Anglophone Beckett studies. As the discipline matured, it became more diverse, and philosophical influence in general – and Cartesianism in particular – gave way to a wave of poststructuralist approaches to Beckett's work in the 1980s and early 1990s. Against the background of this extremely theoretical scholarship, another development was clearly taking shape, namely the growing interest in the archive, with seminal works by Richard Admussen (1979), S. E. Gontarski (1985), Rosemary Pountney (1988), and John Pilling (1999) (among others) emerging as a result.[19] The so-called archival turn, as it is known in present-day Beckett studies, has provided a wealth of material that helps reassess Beckett's engagement with Cartesianism.

(Anti-)Cartesianism in Beckett Studies Today

So what does the archive tell us about Beckett's alleged Cartesianism? Matthew Feldman investigated this question in his study of Beckett's so-called interwar notes (2006). Similarly, Dirk Van Hulle and Mark Nixon scrutinised Beckett's reading traces in his private library in his Paris apartment (2013). Both the library and the notes reveal a much broader spectrum of Beckett's philosophical interests than earlier studies, mostly based on textual interpretation, may have led us to assume.[20]

The history of Beckett's interest in philosophy goes back to the late twenties and early thirties, when the budding writer read voraciously and took a great number of notes in the process. As Knowlson writes in his biography, 'Beckett had been working on philosophy intermittently ever since his Ecole Normale days. He took a great interest in the pre-Socratic philosophers . . . and the problem of the separation of mind and body' (1996, 218). Back then, he also 'read quite a lot about Descartes and the late Cartesians' (219). By contrast, Feldman insists that 'Beckett's knowledge of Cartesian philosophy was superficial and anecdotal' (2006, 46). He believes that 'the "Philosophy Notes" mandate a serious reappraisal of formulations on a "Cartesian Beckett", and simultaneously point to a panorama of

---

[19] See Admussen's 1979 *Samuel Beckett's Manuscripts*, Gontarski's 1985 *The Intent of Undoing*, Pountney's 1988 *Theatre of Shadows* (the latter two both dealing with genetic aspects of Beckett's plays), and Pilling's 1999 *Beckett's Dream Notebook*, to name a few examples.

[20] Of similar design is David Tucker's *Samuel Beckett and Arnold Geulincx* (2012).

philosophical influences based not on a single system or "ism", but on the *system of Western philosophy itself* (39).

Like Knowlson, Feldman traces Beckett's interest in Descartes' philosophy (as opposed to his life as related in *Whoroscope*) to his time at the École normale supérieure and his friendship with Jean Beaufret. The only volume of Descartes' work in Beckett's library is L. Debricon's *Descartes: Choix de Textes*, which Beckett got from Beaufret in 1930 (Feldman, 2006, 47; Van Hulle and Nixon, 2013, 131). The notes and markings in Beckett's copy are most probably Beaufret's (Van Hulle and Nixon 2013, 132), but these could have been used by Beckett as a guideline in the reading process. Debricon's volume contains an eclectic 'mélange' of Descartes' texts, biographical information, and letters, 'subjectively chosen and selectively presented' (Feldman, 2006, 48). Feldman observes that 'there is no evidence of philosophical studies before Beaufret and the Ecole, and no explicit mention of Descartes in Beckett's prose later than *Murphy*'s unspectacular "dream of Descartes linoleum"' (48), although the fact that Descartes' name is not often mentioned does not preclude the presence of his philosophy in Beckett's work. More to the point, Feldman points to Beckett's silence on Descartes in his numerous letters, mostly to MacGreevy, whereas figures such as Geulincx and Schopenhauer are mentioned more than once. In Feldman's view, this indicates Beckett's relative lack of interest in Descartes' work (48–9).

Quite in line with his predilection for 'synoptic overviews' rather than original texts (48), the young Beckett was much influenced by Wilhelm Windelband's *A History of Philosophy* (1901). By comparing excerpts on Descartes in 'Philosophy Notes' to corresponding entries in Windelband, Feldman demonstrates that it was Windelband, and not Descartes' original texts, that served as a source for Beckett's extractions. The same applies to other Cartesians, including Geulincx (at least before Beckett took the trouble of reading Geulincx' original texts in early 1936) and Spinoza.

In the face of the archival evidence, the Cartesian sentiment may have lost its original vigour and become far less ubiquitous, but the idea of Beckett the Cartesian is still very much alive today. A fine example is an article published in 2006 – the same year as Feldman's book – by Dermot Moran, titled 'Beckett and Philosophy' (in a volume dedicated to Beckett's centenary). Forty-five years after *Perspective*'s special issue on Beckett, Moran still claims that 'Beckett did philosophy quite intently, especially in the nineteen twenties and thirties – notably René Descartes, the father of French philosophy' (2006, 97):

> Beckett's characters often make references to Cartesian positions and his
> characters frequently detach from their pains and emotions in order to

comment on them in a dry, analytic manner which makes their calm rationality all the more absurd and disconnected. *His characters actually live through the Cartesian divorce of body from mind.* The body doesn't do what the mind wants. There is a great deal of solipsistic soliloquy especially in the novels, so that one can even speak of *Watt* and other novels as explorations of the disembodied, emotionally detached Cartesian subject. (97; emphasis added)

Such an unequivocal Cartesian reading of Beckett's work, expressed in a recent piece of Beckett scholarship,[21] testifies to the enduring legacy of Cartesianism in Beckett studies. That said, the two most recent essay collections on Beckett and philosophy (Lane's 2002 *Beckett and Philosophy* and Feldman and Mamdani's 2015 *Beckett/Philosophy*) mention Descartes only in passing. This is strikingly different from the first issue of *Perspective* that introduced philosophy in general, and Descartes in particular, as a major influence on Beckett.

The 'anti-Cartesian' developments in Beckett studies today can be roughly divided into three major strands: (1) early Greek philosophy, (2) phenomenology and the body, and (3) postcognitivism. The remainder of this section will be devoted to these developments, placing them in a dialogue with early Beckett scholarship without making judgements or taking sides in this fascinating debate.

Early Greek Philosophy

Famously, when asked about his philosophical influences, Beckett reluctantly imparted the following: 'If I were in the unenviable position of having to study my work my points of departure would be the "Naught is more real . . . " and the "Ubi nihil vales . . . ", both already in *Murphy* and neither very rational'.[22] Many observers have noted the absence of Descartes in the list of Beckett's points of departure, and almost as many have urged not to take Beckett's words too seriously, for fear of them being 'too red a herring' (Beckett, 2010d, 56). However, if we assume that Beckett actually meant what he said, his choice is an interesting one precisely because it is so balanced. With Geulincx, he has chosen the most extreme version of mind/world dualism, and with Democritus, with his monistic atomic theory, he ostensibly opts for the opposite.[23]

---

[21] Moran (2006).

[22] Letter to Sighle Kennedy (1967; Beckett, 1984, 113, also qtd in Feldman, 2006, 153n2). In 1962, Beckett expressed the same idea to Lawrence E. Harvey (qtd in Fifield, 2015, 127).

[23] Democritus' monism is not as straightforward as it may seem at first glance (for details, see Mooney, 1982, 224). What is important for the present discussion is that early Greek thought provided an alternative to the rigid Cartesian mind/world dualism that ostensibly governed Beckett's oeuvre according to early Beckett scholars.

The influence of Democritus – 'oddly neglected' in early Beckett studies, despite Beckett's own confession (Hamilton and Hamilton, 1976, 2–3) – was first invoked by Alice and Kenneth Hamilton back in 1976. Hamilton and Hamilton trace the presence of the 'laughing philosopher' across Beckett's oeuvre, starting with *Dream of Fair to Middling Women* and continuing to Beckett's poems, *Murphy, Watt, Waiting for Godot, Endgame*, the radio plays, the Trilogy, and a number of other texts.[24] Their analysis shows that in most cases Beckett was just as fascinated by the legend of Democritus the person as by his actual philosophy – something we recognise from the way early Beckett studies sketched his relationship with Descartes, in no small measure due to *Whoroscope*.

One of those who took up the Democritean banner, this time openly voicing his intention to go against the grain of Cartesian mainstream in Beckett studies, was Michael Mooney in his 1982 article on *Murphy* and early Greek scepticism. Mooney sets out to 'reassess the Cartesian perspective' on Beckett's work, without, however, disputing the fact that 'Cartesianism is a force in Beckett's writing' (214). Contrary to Mintz, Mooney believes that it is the 'void of nothingness of Democritus' atomism' (218), and not Descartes' dualism, that underlies the third zone of Murphy's mind. Democritus is also present in Molloy's and Malone's storyworlds and resurfaces in *The Unnamable*, in which the hero 'watches all the fictional forms dissolve before him' (218). Also, the image of the kite, featuring so prominently in *Murphy*, receives a Democritean reading in Mooney's analysis, the kite epitomising 'the unseen specks or atomic "motes" discoverable in [the] void' (222).

As in the case of Descartes, Beckett's knowledge of early Greek philosophy in general, and Democritus in particular, came from secondary sources: apart from Windelband, Beckett also consulted John Burnet's *Greek Philosophy: Part I: Thales to Plato* (1915) and Archibald Alexander's *A Short History of Philosophy* (1922). Van Hulle and Nixon also mention Friedrich Ueberweg's *History of Philosophy: From Thales to the Present Time* (2013, 129).[25] That said, their research also shows that, unlike Descartes' original work (consisting solely of Debricon's highly selective *Choix de textes*), early Greek thought is represented by a number of French-language volumes in Beckett's Paris library: 'even after the Second World War, new acquisitions in Beckett's library keep showing traces of [his] interest in the Presocratics, up until the year before the author's death' (2013,

---

[24] Feldman notes that 'writing against dominant Cartesian readings in Beckett Studies, the Hamiltons are to be commended for suggesting that Beckett's knowledge of Presocratic thought was evident in both his interwar and postwar texts' (2006, 60).

[25] Peter Fifield (2015) convincingly demonstrates the hitherto underrated importance of Ueberweg's book for Beckett's study of early Greek thought, especially of Thales, Anaximenes, and Anaximander.

128). Since these books contain no marginalia, it is not clear whether Beckett has ever read them. If he did, this would have been done at a later stage of his life, long after the period of his intensive acquisition of knowledge in the thirties.

In his attempt to defend the pre-Socratic cause, Feldman provides a survey of Democritean themes in Beckett's work. Apart from labelling *Murphy* 'a Democritean' rather than Cartesian novel, he mentions the pairing of Democritus and Heraclitus in *More Pricks Than Kicks* ('if only anecdotally and without reference to their philosophical ideas'; 60), as well as the evocation of Democritus in *Malone Dies* (already much more oblique, about 'Nothing is more real than nothing' being 'one of those phrases that seem so innocuous and, once you let them in, pollute the whole of speech'; 60). In *The Unnamable*, Democritus is mentioned in person, once again paired with Heraclitus, albeit in a twisted, Beckettian way, with the reference even more obscured:

> I'll laugh, that's how it will end, in a chuckle, . . . I'll practice, . . . nothing but emotion, bing bang, . . . that's love, enough, it's tiring, hee hee, that's the Abderite, no, the other, in the end, it's the end, the ending end . . . open on the void, open on the nothing. I've no objection, those are words, open on the silence, looking out on the silence . . . (Beckett, 2010d, 127)

In the closing section of *Texts for Nothing*, the Democritean laugh is mentioned again: 'here the laugh, the long silent guffaw of the knowing non-exister, at hearing ascribed to him such pregnant words' (Beckett, 2010c, 50, also qtd in Feldman, 2006, 61). Once again, as in *The Unnamable*, it is Democritus' personal feature – his 'guffaw' – that is foregrounded.

Feldman's crusade against Cartesianism in Beckett studies is powered to a large extent by archival research. The next example of anti-Cartesian scholarship takes a different approach: having little archival evidence to corroborate her theory, Ulrika Maude nonetheless makes a solid case for the influence of phenomenology on Beckett's treatment of the body in his work.[26]

Phenomenology and the Body

Maude's comprehensive investigation focuses on the materiality of the body in Beckett's texts. Although the omnipresence of the body throughout Beckett's oeuvre has long been recognised,

---

[26] The very fact that Maude succeeds in debunking the Cartesian reading of Beckett's work in favour of the phenomenological one without drawing on Beckett's notebooks or reading traces indicates that Feldman's reliance on the archive and Karl Popper's falsifiability theory are not the only ways to argue the anti-Cartesian case in Beckett scholarship. For all its soundness of evidence, the archive also harbours gaps and lacunae, often undetected and therefore easily overlooked (cf. the Feldman–Gowd debate on this highly contested subject in *Samuel Beckett Today/Aujourd'hui* 20 (2008, 375–99).

crucial aspects of its pronounced status in Beckett's work have remained unaddressed. The first wave of Beckett scholarship ... read Beckett as a transcendental writer who subscribed to a Cartesian dualism. The prominence of the body and its decrepitude was accredited to the body's inherent otherness; what truly mattered in Beckett was the mind and its capacity to move beyond matter. (Maude, 2009, 1)

Kenner's 'Cartesian Centaur', for instance, emphasises 'the imperfection of the body, which pales in the light of the superiority of the rationally constructed bicycle. The body and its surroundings, in this view, are read as little more than obstacles' (2). Such a 'one-dimensional reading', Maude claims, is not just 'reductive'; it also – and more importantly – ignores 'the centrality of sensory perception in Beckett's work' (2).

Maude notes that in Beckett studies, 'the problem of representation is privileged over experience' (3). She attempts to redress this imbalance by going back to 'the very basics of bodily existence, those conditions that are already in swing *before* culture lays its mark on embodied identity' (2). True to her intentions, she goes on to explore the 'prereflective physicality' (4) in Beckett's work – that is, vision, hearing, tactile perception, and basic motility. Her theoretical framework is the phenomenology of Maurice Merleau-Ponty, whose theories have also been foundational for enactivism in cognitive science and philosophy.[27] Crucially for Maude's purposes, Merleau-Ponty 'stressed what he called the "primacy" of perception, foregrounding the importance of prereflective experience to our encounter with the world' (4–5).

Maude's investigation emphasises the role of the body as a depository of memories (as in *Proust* and *Krapp's Last Tape*), as well as the characters' sense of 'being in the world': 'Despite the transcendentalist claims of early humanist readings of Beckett's work, critics now widely concur that the Beckettian characters' experience of the world is a markedly physical, bodily experience. Whether we are dealing with prose or drama, it is the body, rather than the *cogito*, that gives the characters assurance of their existence' (10). A good example of such bodily experience of the world is to be found in the opening lines of *Company*, in which 'the narrated character is lying on his back in the dark, listening to a voice. He is aware of this "by the pressure on his hind parts and by how the dark changes when he shuts his eyes and again when he opens them again"' (Beckett, 2009a, 3, qtd in Maude, 2009, 10). For a text seemingly devoid of so-called embodied action due to its focus on (interior) imagination,

---

[27] Of all phenomenologists of his generation, Merleau-Ponty was most concerned with what we now call 'embodied cognition': he believed that 'instead of being an object in the world, the body ... forms the foundation of all forms of human experience' (Maude, 2009, 4).

such foregrounding of the body's unmediated connection to the mind is noteworthy.

In her discussion of vision, Maude uses *Film* as a case in point. *Film* 'is important from two points of view: firstly, because it focuses on the question of the subject as the object of perception; and secondly, because the mode of representation is restricted almost purely to the visual' (41). Although the script did originally contain various sounds, the end result was a silent film. The elimination of sound only increases the film's focus on vision – in particular the gaze, both of the perceiver (E, or the Eye) and the perceived (O, or the Object). Maude notes how '*Film* emblematically opens and closes with a close-up of [Buster] Keaton's veiny, bloodshot eye and its wrinkled, shiny lid, which emphasizes the physical, fleshy nature of sight' (42). The crux of the script is, as Beckett put it, a 'search for non-being in flight from extraneous perception breaking down in inescapability of self-perception' (qtd in Maude, 2009, 45), which puts Berkeley's famous dictum (and the first line of the script) in a different light. Essentially a radical dualist statement, *esse est percipi* becomes in this case the proof of quite the opposite, as being is grounded in ineluctable, ineliminable *self*-perception. In other words, in *Film*, to be perceived *is* to perceive, and vice versa. The inherent duality of the observer and the observed is thus eradicated, meaning that *Film* 'disavows the possibility of a separation of the self from the world' (45):

> Because of self-perception, it becomes impossible for O to extricate himself from the picture, whether here understood as the frame, the film or the world. If autonomy is based on the fact that the subject is the *agent* rather than the *object* of perception, by focusing perception on the self, Becket collapses the categorical distinction and shatters the illusion of autonomous subjectivity ... The eye situates the subject in the world rather than detaches it from its surroundings. (46)

Considering Beckett's oeuvre in general (and probably with his later work in mind), Maude observes that '[e]ven in the sensory deprivation of the barren spaces they inhabit, ... the characters continue to interact with their surroundings, or to create phantom landscapes with which to interact when actual landscapes are no longer to be found' (46).

Even more than the trope of vision, early critics treated sound in Beckett's fiction 'as a marker of interiority' (Maude, 2009, 47). This additional bias has much to do with Beckett's radio plays, which have been seen as the perfect expression of a 'disembodied' voice in Beckett's work (47). The general line in early Beckett scholarship was that 'Beckett turned to the radio medium ... because it offered him the most effective means of portraying a character's mind, which humanist critics have considered the author's main objective' (47). Martin Esslin, whose work on Beckett and radio still belong to the canon of Beckett scholarship on the subject of media and technology, wrote in 1971 that 'it is through the ear that *words* are primarily communicated; and words communicate concepts, thought, information on a more abstract level than the images of the world the eye takes in' (qtd in Maude, 2009, 47; emphasis added).[28] In Esslin's view, radio 'allowed Beckett to eliminate much that was superfluous in his work, in favour of a privileged interiority' (Maude, 2009, 48). Similarly, Clas Zilliacus, another household name as far as Beckett's radio plays are concerned, saw the radio medium as 'nonspatial and uncorporeal' (1976, qtd in Maude, 2009, 48). These characteristics have set the tone for subsequent studies of Beckett's radio plays: the main idea was that 'the radio enabled the kind of disembodiment that Beckett had been seeking in his writings' (48). Regarding in particular the first two plays, *All That Fall* and *Embers*, and despite the abundance of environmental sounds, critics have shown a consistent bias towards interiority, as Maude convincingly demonstrates.[29] As an alternative interpretation, Maude suggests that

> Beckett's prolific use of sound in *All That Fall* goes against the essentially speech-based tradition of radio drama. It also renders problematic the claims about the play's focus on interiority and language. A close reading of the play that takes into account the phenomenology of sound and hearing will suggest that *All That Fall* prioritizes exteriority and matter over interiority and the problems of conceptual thought. (49)

Though one might question Maude's final point, it is difficult to ignore environmental noises that abound in the play. Moreover, the play is packed with non-verbal action, including visual and tactile elements, and is situated within an identifiable spatiotemporal environment:

> Instead of being nonspatial, . . . *All That Fall* uses sound's spatializing quality to evoke a vivid and multidimensional topography. By relying on sound, the play paradoxically only emphasizes the situatedness and facticity of its

---

[28] It is noteworthy that Esslin refers to words rather than sounds, which seems to contradict Beckett's own lamentations on language, especially English, being 'abstracted to death', already expressed in 1937 in his letter to Axel Kaun (cf. *LSB I*, 515). It is just possible, then, that Beckett's turn to radio was motivated by his desire to move *away* from the dead abstraction of the (written) word and explore the lived, physical phenomenon of sound instead.

[29] In Maude's overview of critical reactions to *All That Fall* (2009, 49), which, as well as Esslin, includes such scholars as Katharine Worth, Linda Ben-Zvi, and Everett Frost, expressions such as 'Maddy's mind', 'inner landscape', 'world that exists within the skull', and 'within the mind of Maddy Rooney' give a fair impression of the direction the play's criticism has taken. Ruby Cohn considered the play to foreground language (i.e., the abstracted, conceptual level), and Zilliacus went even further by claiming that *All That Fall* is 'all about language' (qtd in Maude, 2009, 49).

characters. Similarly, the play's emphasis on the predicament of the body on the levels of story . . ., formal structure . . ., plot . . . and thematic content . . . reveals the play's insistent focus on exteriority and the embodied nature of subjectivity. (Maude, 2009, 56)[30]

Perhaps the most essential point in the discussion is Maude's distinction between visual and auditory perception: 'the sense of hearing, because sounds "penetrate us from all directions at all times" (Rodaway, 1994), places the subject *within* a world rather than *in front of one* as vision does' (Maude, 2009, 51; emphasis added).[31] Thus, auditory input, especially emanating from radio (rather than from a clearly visible source), is much less 'dualist' and 'representational', because the listener is right in the middle of it, surrounded, as it were, by an array of sounds coming literally out of thin air, with no corresponding visual object to pin them down to.

Even more than *All That Fall*, in the early criticism *Embers* has been associated with isolation and interiority. In particular, Hugh Kenner believed that '*Embers* locks the listener "inside the word spinner's prison"' (1961, qtd in Maude, 2009, 56), whereas 'John Fletcher and John Spurling conclude that "the world of . . . Henry is firmly interiorized, since the sounds he hears (and we hear) are mainly in his head"' (1972, qtd in Maude, 2009, 56). Similarly, Zilliacus claims that *Embers* portrays 'one man's world: the interplay between Henry and other characters takes place in Henry's mind' (1976, qtd in Maude, 2009, 56), and Esslin agrees that 'the voices are all internal' (1986, qtd in Maude, 2009, 56). The list goes on, but the verdict issued by the critical mainstream is crystal clear: in *Embers*, action is fully interiorised and takes place solely in Henry's head. However, this surprising consensus does not seem to take into account Beckett's own admission of the play's inherent ambiguity, which was the reason why a stage adaptation was out of the question: '*Embers* relies on ambiguity: are the characters hallucinations or are they real? A scenic realization would destroy the ambiguity' (qtd in Maude, 2009, 57). Another important issue is

---

[30] It seems that those critics who pointed to the play's alleged inwardness also noticed its 'richer-than-usual realism' (Worth 1981, 193) and its 'verbal concreteness, a defined locale, and a larger cast than any other of Beckett's plays save . . . *Eleuthéria*' (Zilliacus 1976, 30). Therefore, '[t]here is . . . an inconsistency between various critics' emphasis on interiority and their simultaneous stress on the play's realism and day-to-day topography. Not only is the play spatially specific; the material world it constructs is so forceful that it finds its way into the critical commentary' (Maude, 2009, 51).

[31] Maude's formulation recalls Beckett's own phrasing in his 1949 letter to Georges Duthuit, in which he states that as an artist he is incapable of being 'in front of' the object of his art (*LSB II*, 140). The Duthuit letter will be key to our discussion of Beckett's own views on subject/object relations in Section 2.

the importance of the dual nature of the sonorous space, which consists of sounds emitted by the subject and other sounds that originate in the environment surrounding the subject. The envelope of sound, like the skin, hence embodies a dialectic between interiority and exteriority, epitomized, perhaps, in the tympanum of the ear, which itself consists of a skin. (Maude, 2009, 57)[32]

In other words, even if we assume that (on the story level) everything is happening inside Henry's mind, the way the mind is portrayed (on the discourse level) – so full of environmental sounds, with the sound of the sea being of paramount importance – points to a constitutive role of both the sound as a physical, material phenomenon and the environment that contains sound in shaping Henry's fictional mind.

Extended Cognition

The issue that Maude raises – about the boundary between the inside and the outside – further illustrates the arbitrariness of such a boundary, especially regarding such an evanescent and ephemeral phenomenon as sound. To paraphrase Clark and Chalmers' foundational question, where does the outside end and the inside begin? The same question underlies Dirk Van Hulle's pioneering research on Beckett and extended cognition (2012, 2014a). Another postcognitivist approach (like Maude's), it focuses less on embodiment and more on the way the brain – be it the author's or the character's – interacts with its environment, relying (like the present study) on enactivism and the extended mind theory as a theoretical framework.

From the outset, Van Hulle remarks that '[t]he image of the mind as an "inside", contrasted with an "outside," is based on the Cartesian model of the mind as an interior space, which is becoming increasingly implausible due to recent developments in cognitive science' (2012, 277). Recognising that the Cartesian and Geulingian mind/world split underlies much of Beckett's work, if only for the purposes of parodying them, Van Hulle notes its lasting impact on Beckett's prose works:

> The Chinese-boxes effect of the homunculus model,[33] with its infinite *mise-en-abyme* structure, also aligns with the model of the M-characters and narrators in Beckett's post-war novels, notably *Mercier et Camier*, *Molloy*, *Malone Dies* and *The Unnamable*. The last paragraph of the preamble in *The*

---

[32] This invokes the Unnamable's reference to himself as the tympanum (Beckett, 2010d, 100), which will be discussed in detail in Section 2.

[33] According to Descartes, a homunculus is a little creature inside the pineal gland (the place in the brain where mind and body meet) that is supposedly responsible for centrally managing all our perceptual and cognitive activity.

Unnamable opens with the enumeration of the first-person narrator's predecessors: 'All these Murphys, Molloys and Malones do not fool me' (*U* 14).
The narrator then devises a few stories and characters that are referred to as
'avatars', with names like Basil, Mahood and Worm. . . . The use of the word
'homuncules' (already in the preceding novel, *Malone meurt / Malone Dies*)
reinforces the hypothesis that – five novels after *Murphy* – Beckett was still
struggling with the Cartesian model. (2014a, 189)[34]

It is precisely this struggle, i.e. the realisation that Cartesianism (in whatever
form) is not the answer, that entices Beckett to continue his attempts to 'eff the
ineffable' and 'keep looking for other models to investigate how our body is
moved by the mind and how the mind is moved by our body and by bodies
existing outside us' (Van Hulle, 2012, 281). In his quest, Beckett may have
intuitively hit upon the principle of extended cognition, as elements of both
enactivism and the extended mind theory can be traced in his texts (Van Hulle,
2012, 2014a).

For an illustrative example, Van Hulle turns to Beckett's late short text
'Ceiling', which 'is about the slow process of regaining consciousness, or
"coming to" as it is called in the text' (2014a, 206). Both the story and the
storyworld are reduced to a bare minimum, being about 'a man lying in a bed,
opening his eyes. The first thing he sees is the white ceiling: "On coming to his
first sight was of white"' (Beckett, 2009a, 129, qtd in Van Hulle, 2014a, 206).
The slow awakening of the man's consciousness is continuously triggered by
the ceiling he is seeing, with its 'dull white' colour being a point of reference
throughout the text. As Van Hulle notes,

> It is remarkable that, in this patient study of the dimly conscious mind,
> Beckett describes its workings by means of the interaction with an external
> object, the white ceiling. Not unlike the interaction between the intelligent
> agent and the wall in Woolf's story 'The Mark on the Wall' . . ., the mind is
> explicitly extended to an external environment. Although this environment is
> deliberately reduced to just a ceiling, it does play an active role in driving the
> cognitive process of coming to. (2014a, 207)[35]

In Virginia Woolf's story (1917), a long stream of consciousness is unleashed on
the reader, suggesting an exclusively inward nature of the narrator's mind. Yet,
as Van Hulle notes, the trigger for that ostensibly brain-bound cognitive activity
is an external object, the mark on the wall that catches the narrator's eye on three

---

[34] Marco Bernini also discusses the homunculus model in his postcognitivist reading of the
Unnamable (2014).

[35] It may indeed be argued that the fewer objects the storyworld contains, the more important they
are for the story and the greater their role in activating the fictional mind's cognitive activity, as
we shall see in Section 2.

occasions in the story, making the ensuing cognitive process an extended one (see Van Hulle, 2014a, 142–9). Both in 'Ceiling' and 'The Mark on the Wall', instead of being described or represented, consciousness is enacted in and by the text (2014a, 207).

Whereas the role of Descartes' dualist doctrine was excessively fore-grounded in early Anglophone Beckett scholarship, later studies covered a much broader spectrum of his philosophical influences, diminishing – though by no means eliminating – the Cartesian angle and opening other lines of enquiry, often based on documental evidence to support their arguments. While Cartesian 'emblems' (to use Morot-Sir's elegant term) never quite disappeared from Beckett's oeuvre, one cannot fail to notice the increasing emphasis on the materiality and embodiment in Beckett's texts in present-day Beckett scholarship, a development that goes hand in hand with the growing popularity of archival research and a genetic approach to Beckett's work. Section 2 will continue to subvert the 'critical commonplace' of 'skullscapes' and 'soulscapes'[36] in Beckett studies by drawing on examples from Beckett's prose that point instead to the Beckettian mind grounded in hybrid cognitive activity (i.e., continuously and constitutively interacting with its fictional environment).

2 Extended Cognition in Beckett's Prose

This section aims to discuss Beckett's fictional minds from the vantage point of extended cognition. What it does *not* aim to do is create a postcognitivist bias for Beckett's oeuvre in the process of nuancing the Cartesian one. Instead, the objective is to engage with early and contemporary Beckett criticism by approaching Beckett's work from a different angle. This way, both the dualist (Cartesian) and postcognitivist (anti-Cartesian) perspectives can be compared and contrasted, without either of them being foregrounded as a better fit for the Beckettian universe.[37]

---

[36] The term 'soulscape' was coined by Ruby Cohn (1980, 82).

[37] Briefly zooming out of Beckett scholarship, it is noteworthy that postcognitivism was introduced to literary studies as a means to reassess the so-called modernist 'inward turn'. In his 2011 article 'Re-minding Modernism', David Herman questions the ubiquitous representation of the modernist fictional mind as an exclusively 'interior space', and disputes its exploration as 'a movement inwards' (248) and 'prob[ing of] psychological depths' (249). Instead, Herman argues that 'modernist narratives can both be illuminated by and help illuminate postcognitivist accounts of the mind as inextricably embedded in contexts for action and interaction' (249). By linking modernist fiction to 'externalist' theories of cognition, Herman suggests that, contrary to common assumption, 'the [Modernist] mind does not reside within; instead, it emerges through humans' dynamic interdependence with the social and material environment they seek to navigate' (254). For a more detailed discussion of the modernist 'inward turn' and Herman's take on it, see Beloborodova 2018.

Beckett's extended and enactive fictional minds will be discussed on two levels – the level of story and the level of discourse – with occasional excursions into the level of composition. By now deeply entrenched in literary studies, the story/discourse bifurcation was theorised in 1978 by Seymour Chatman, who defined it as follows: '[A] story (histoire) [is] the content or chain of events (actions, happenings), plus what may be called the existents (characters, items of setting); and a discourse (discours) [is] the expression, the means by which the content is communicated. In simple terms, the story is the *what* in a narrative that is depicted, discourse the *how*' (1978, 19). As most Beckett scholars would agree, 'the *what* in a narrative' in Beckett's work gradually disappears in the course of his long writing career in favour of 'the *how*', with the borderline between the two becoming increasingly porous and dissipating altogether in the later works. Consequently, in Beckett's early prose the story element occupies a more dominant position (as indeed it should in a more traditional narrative) and contains a heterodiegetic third-person narrator (albeit not so omniscient and far from invisible), a more or less chronological plot, and a number of characters interacting with one another. Fictional minds in such narratives inevitably have a number of different action possibilities, which facilitates their analysis from the action-oriented externalist vantage point. This is why the *extended mind thesis*, which presupposes an interaction between the neural brain and objects in the external world, will be of particular importance in the discussion of the early works.

As Beckett's oeuvre matures, the story element diminishes in terms of action, characters, and setting. The postwar switch to first-person narration, together with Beckett's decision to implement the 'less is more' principle in his writing, are the two arguments that could be (and indeed have been) used to advocate Beckett's own 'inward turn', with the Trilogy's protagonists ostensibly leaving the world behind and retreating more into the realm of their minds. However, a closer look at the texts reveals a different picture: even if his later works contain less of the world (in the 'big blooming buzzing confusion' sense of the word), the mind still finds or otherwise devises something to continuously interact with, for company or otherwise. Instead of registering a move inwards, what the present section will lay bare is a *postcognitivist continuum*: as mind and world intermingle in Beckett's later works, the inside/outside opposition fades and dissolves almost completely. In the end, it loses the relevance it still had in his earlier oeuvre, which calls for an *enactive* rather than extended account of the way fictional minds continuously shape and are being shaped by their often immaterial environment.

Throughout this section, a number of parameters will be used to detect extended cognitive activity in Beckett's fictional minds: from objects, spatiotemporal anchoring, and people in the early work we move to intertexts, voices, and language in the later texts (elements less material but by no means less extracranial). Needless to say, this is a much too schematic presentation, designed only to reflect the main tendency of the section's development: intertextuality, for one, will also play a part in the early prose, and spatial markers such as place names will return on occasion in later works.

Before we move on to Beckett's fictional minds proper, is important to point out that the continuum principle outlined above does not entail the notion of improvement or progress. What this section by no means aspires to do is to present a 'better' alternative to Cartesianism, or to show how Beckett, having dispensed with the mind/world dualist thought system, has finally discovered a perfect alternative to it in his later works. As we shall see, the evolution of Cartesian oppositions in Beckett's prose is all but linear, and Cartesian imagery (if only as an aesthetic tool) will remain a force to be reckoned with throughout Beckett's work.

Story: Extended Mind

The dualist inside/outside opposition and the related story/discourse distinction preoccupied Beckett from the very start of his writing career. As early as 1929, Beckett admired Joyce's modus operandi in 'Work in Progress': 'Here form is content, content is form. ... His writing is not about something; it is that something itself. ... Where the sense is sleep, the words go to sleep. ... Where the sense is dancing, the words dance' (Beckett, 1984, 27). In *Proust* (1931), Beckett reiterated this sentiment: 'Proust does not share the superstition that form is nothing and content everything .... Indeed he makes no attempt to dissociate form from content. The one is a concretion of the other, the revelation of the world' (Beckett, 1965, 88). What Beckett seems to reject in both cases is storytelling as a representational account – that is, the existence of a pre-given tale to be told or a pre-given world to be apprehended by an autonomous subject (in this case, the artist). Instead, he advocates Joyce's strategy of literary enactment. In 'Recent Irish Poetry' (1934), Beckett praised 'the poets who have turned their backs on the "bankrupt relationship" between subject and object, language and world, and accepted the aesthetic obligation in their poetry to "state the space" between inner and outer worlds, and between word and object' (Weller, 2018, 38). The space in between is something that will continue to fascinate Beckett throughout his career, and resurfaces in his more mature critical observations in 'Three Dialogues with Georges Duthuit' (1949) and his Duthuit correspondence.

More Pricks Than Kicks *(1934)*

The neatness of the inside/outside opposition is already subverted in the very first lines of the first story in *More Pricks Than Kicks*. This is how 'Dante and the Lobster' begins:

> It was midnight, and Belacqua was stuck in the first of the canti in the moon.
> He was so bogged that he could move neither backward nor forward. Blissful
> Beatrice was there, Dante also, and she explained the spots on the moon to
> him. . . . All he had to do was to follow her step by step. (Beckett 2010a, 3)

Here, readers are thrown into the story *in medias res* and have to think twice
before they realise that the narrator is describing the reading process of the
protagonist. The total immersion of Belacqua in the *Divina Commedia* (being
literally 'stuck in' the text) reflects the tight cognitive coupling between the
fictional reader's brain and the external object the text represents, and the
bewildered *real* readers of the story share Belacqua's predicament in a very
straightforward way, being equally 'stuck' and 'bogged' while reading those
lines. Add to this the name of the protagonist, coming straight from the *Divina
Commedia* itself, and the reader's confusion is complete.

Throughout the story, Belacqua desperately tries to isolate himself from the
outside world, but continuously fails to do so. In his attempt to attain 'tranquil-
lity' in his mind and to concentrate on preparing lunch, he tries to keep the
outside world away: 'The first thing to do was to lock the door. Now nobody
could come at him' (Beckett, 2010a, 4). However, despite the door being
locked, the outside world does find a way to get to Belacqua in the very next
sentence: 'He deployed an old *Herald* and smoothed it out on the table. The
rather handsome face of McCabe the assassin stared up at him' (4). The
subsequent description of toasting the bread is permeated with references to
the alleged Malahide murderer:[38] the loaf being 'evened off on the face of
McCabe', the superfluous part of the bread going 'back into prison', the 'soft of
the bread' being first 'warm, alive' and then 'done to a dead end' (4–5). McCabe
will return in the closing section of the story:

> Where we were, thought Belacqua, as we were.[39] He walked on, gripping his
> parcel. Why not piety and pity both, even down below?[40] Why not mercy and
> Godliness together? A little mercy in the stress of sacrifice, a little mercy to
> rejoice against judgment? He thought of Jonah and the gourd and the pity of
> a jealous God of Nineveh. And poor McCabe, he would get it in the neck at
> dawn. What was he doing now, how was he feeling? He would relish one more
> meal, one more night. (Beckett, 2010a, 13)

---

[38] A highly publicised murder case that would have been familiar to the contemporary reader; for
details, see Kroll, 1977. As Pilling notes, 'the story connects Dante, McCabe and the lobster'
(2011, 55) – all external and completely different elements.

[39] Even these words are not Belacqua's: they were uttered by the pensive and melancholic Signora
Ottolenghi during their Italian lesson.

[40] A reference to the 'superb pun' from Dante that Belacqua wants Ottolenghi to translate during
their lesson: 'qui vive la pietà quando è ben morta'. Ottolenghi, however, declines the request
(Beckett, 2010a, 11–12).

In this instance, Belacqua is clearly absorbed in thought and oblivious to what is going on around him (he is walking to his aunt's house carrying the lobster), which generates a purely internal cognitive activity. However, it is remarkable that Belacqua's consciousness in its ostensibly unextended state is so packed with external elements: apart from McCabe, there is Dante and the Bible, as well as Ottolenghi's words. Even in the depths of his thoughts, Belacqua's mind can't help but extend into the universe it inhabits – his books, his lesson, and current affairs all intermingle in his musings.

Murphy *(1938)*

The focus on the mind/world separation continues and intensifies in *Murphy*. Famously labelled Cartesian by early critics (as we saw above), the novel is grounded – in terms of both its form and its content – in the mind/world opposition and portrays Murphy's desperate and failing struggle to live in his mind and escape from the world. Moreover, the mind in *Murphy* is unequi-vocally and consistently represented as a self-contained, autonomous entity, 'hermetically closed to the universe without' (Beckett, 2009c, 69), and the separation between Murphy on the one hand and the rest of the characters on the other is constantly underscored ('All the puppets in this book whinge sooner or later, except Murphy, who is not a puppet' (78)). Even Murphy's suit is described as 'entirely non-porous. It admitted no air from the outer world, it allowed none of Murphy's own vapours to escape' (47). With these points in mind, one may wonder if there is a case to be made at all for extended cognition in a book that insists so bluntly on rigid subject/object dualism, even if the intention was to parody the Cartesian doctrine rather than defend it. However, Murphy's profound embedding in the city of London (with the floor of a London pub featuring as his last resting place), his disappointment in the 'little world' of Mr Endon, and his non-abating desire for Celia and ginger biscuits all serve to undermine the dogma of Murphy as 'an orthodox Cartesian' (Mintz, 1959, 157).

The most obvious example of Murphy's deep anchoring in the material world of objects is his interaction with his rocking chair, which he uses to attain a certain state of mind:

> He sat naked in his rocking-chair of undressed teak . . . It was his, it never left him. Seven scarves held him in position. . . . Only the most local movements were possible. . . . Somewhere a cuckoo-clock, having struck between twenty and thirty, became the echo of a street-cry, which now entering the mew gave *Quid pro quo! Quid pro quo!* directly. (Beckett, 2009c, 3)

The purpose of this strange exercise was to attain a state of contemplation, far removed from the 'big world' to which Murphy felt he did not belong, and enter the 'little world' of his mind, but the process was a laborious one. He first had to filter out the environmental 'sights and sounds' ('He wondered dimly what was breaking up his sunlight, what wares were being cried' (3)), and then 'appease ... his body. ... For it was not until his body was appeased that he could come alive in his mind ... And life in his mind gave him pleasure, such pleasure that pleasure was not the word' (4). Even when everything finally went according to plan, the outside world kept interfering:

> He worked up the chair to its maximum rock, then relaxed. Slowly the world died down, the big world where *Quid pro quo* was cried as wares and the light never waned the same way twice; in favour of the little, ... where he could love himself.
>   A foot from his ear the telephone burst into its rail. (Beckett, 2009c, 6)

This episode exemplifies Murphy's attempts to retreat into his 'little world' by means of his rocking chair, while the 'big world' constantly manifests itself in one way or another. Whereas Mintz invokes the chair as 'best suited' for Murphy to complete his Cartesian self-isolation (1959; see the discussion of Mintz' article above), it is precisely this constitutive (i.e., indispensable) relationship that makes this mundane object part of Murphy's extended cognitive system. By manipulating this object in a particular way, he attains a certain *state of mind* – in other words, this is not simply a physical reaction to the bondage and the rocking. Although the purpose of this extended system is to sever rather than boost the connection between the mind and the 'big world', the principle of extended cognition still applies, as an external tool is used to enable (or, in this case, disable) cognitive activity. Another condition that satisfies the criterion for an extended cognitive system is that the chair is always within Murphy's reach and can be used for that purpose whenever necessary.

Molloy *(1951)*

If objects, people, and topographical details dominate the *Murphy* universe, the situation in *Molloy* is quite different. As O'Reilly, Van Hulle, and Verhulst note in their introduction to *The Making of* Molloy (2017), the novel's composition occurs in 'a period of two turnings, one from [Beckett's] mother tongue to writing in a new language, the other from early work that left him unsatisfied to the prolonged exploration of impoverishment, impotence and ignorance' (25). A third 'turning', possibly a direct consequence of the second, is from third-person to first-person narration – a change that will entail the foregrounding of the Cartesian 'I', or 'the cursed first-person pronoun', as the Unnamable will ominously refer to it (Beckett 2010d, 56).[41] This consequence of the switch to first-person narration will become increasingly pertinent as the discourse element within the narrative grows in relevance in Beckett's subsequent works.

Describing the change in Beckett's writing style that precipitated *Molloy*, James Knowlson uses the dualist language that has become part and parcel of Beckett criticism: from that point onwards, Beckett

> would draw . . . on his own inner world for his subjects; outside reality would be refracted through the filter of his own imagination; inner desires and needs would be allowed a much greater freedom of expression; rational contradictions would be allowed in; and the imagination would be allowed to create alternative worlds to those of conventional reality. (1996, 352)

Although Knowlson certainly has a point, the picture he presents can be nuanced from the vantage point of extended cognition. First of all, the emphasis on the shift of focus to the 'inner world' does not necessarily preclude the presence of the world at large, even if that world is less 'realist' than it was in *Murphy*. The very structure of the novel, both parts of it being quest narratives, implies at least some form of action within the storyworld: both Molloy and Moran (as experiencing selves) are on a journey, making their way through a forest, encountering other people, constantly getting themselves in and out of trouble – all of this action interspersed, admittedly, by numerous elaborations and musings of a clearly internal nature. These musings are accompanied by many meta-comments from the narrators (both Molloy and Moran), and one of them is particularly interesting for the present enquiry. Elaborating on the nature of his seemingly isolated mind in Lousse's garden, Molloy admits that sometimes he and the garden became one, and he was 'no longer *that sealed jar* to which I owed my being so well preserved, but a wall gave way and *I filled with roots and tame stems* for example, stakes long since dead and ready for burning, the recess of night and the imminence of dawn' (Beckett, 2009b, 48; emphasis added). Here, we catch a glimpse of how the independent Cartesian mind, the 'sealed jar' surrounded by a wall, unravels and merges, albeit for a short while, with its living, organic environment (as opposed to the 'dead', inorganic quality of the jar and the wall as enclosures of that mind).[42] Even though, by Molloy's own admission, such mingling was a rare occurrence (implying that the dualist model of the mind still dominates), this explicit reference to the wall of the

---

[41] Although the switch in narration occurred for the first time in the four novellas, *Molloy* was Beckett's first longer piece of prose that deployed the 'I'-narrator.

[42] John Fletcher discusses the same passage from a strictly Cartesian angle (1964, 144), but fails to pick up on the suggestion that on occasion the jar will have cracks and let the world in. Yoshiki Tajiri also mentions it in his discussion (albeit from a predominantly psychoanalytical angle) of the ambiguity of bodily boundaries in Beckett's work (2007, 55).

Cartesian mind giving way foreshadows the gradual yet irrevocable dissolution
of the cogito's shell of Molloy's successors.

One such crack in Molloy's 'jar' is the sucking stones episode, which
illustrates Molloy's extended mind at work in one of his rare moments of
interaction with objects in his storyworld. From an extended cognitive perspective, the sucking stones episode reveals a nexus between the protagonist's brain
and his environment. It demonstrates how the manipulation of objects (even
simple ones like pebbles) can enhance the brain's cognitive ability to solve what
is in this case a mathematical problem.[43] The whole passage, in a true Wattean
fashion, occupies several pages in the book. The following is just a short excerpt
to show how extended cognitive action is portrayed:

> I took advantage of being at the seaside to lay in a store of sucking-stones. . . .
> I distributed them equally between my four pockets, and sucked them turn
> and turn about. This raised a problem which I first solved in the following
> way. I had say sixteen stones, four in each of my four pockets, there being the
> two pockets of my trousers and the two pockets of my greatcoat. Taking
> a stone from the right pocket of my greatcoat, and putting it into my mouth,
> I replaced it in the right pocket of greatcoat by a stone from the right pocket of
> my trousers, which I replaced by a stone from the left pocket of my trousers,
> which I replaced by a stone from the left pocket of my greatcoat, which
> I replaced by the stone which was in my mouth, as soon as I had finished
> sucking it. (Beckett, 2009b, 69)

Molloy's physical manipulation of the stones as part of the solution to his
distribution problem is similar to Andy Clark's Tetris argument, in which he
suggests that playing the game by actually moving about the pieces is much
easier than performing these manipulations in the head (Clark and Chalmers,
2010, 28). Besides, the way Molloy presents his 'extended' solution is also
remarkable:

> Now I can begin to suck. *Watch me closely.* I take a stone from the right
> pocket of my greatcoat, suck it, stop sucking it, put it in the left pocket of my
> greatcoat, the one empty (of stones). I take a second stone from the right
> pocket of my greatcoat, suck it, put it in the left pocket of my greatcoat. And
> so on until the right pocket of my greatcoat is empty . . . and the six stones
> I have just sucked, one after the other, are all in the left pocket of my
> greatcoat. Pausing then, and concentrating, so as not to make a balls of it,
> I transfer to the right pocket, in which there are no stones left, the five stones
> in the right pocket of my trousers, . . . (Beckett, 2009b, 72–3; emphasis
> added)

---

[43] Paul Sheehan also notes the passage – if only in passing – in his article on Beckett's work and the
extended mind: 'Active externalism, for example, can be seen with Molloy and his sucking
stones, which facilitate his permutative deliberations' (2017, 141).

Having endured a long dive into Molloy's psyche during his musings on the best possible solution to his stones problem, the reader is suddenly prompted by the imperative 'Watch me closely' to conjure up a scene – in the present tense, so in the here and now – of a very physical, embodied process, being propelled to a position right next to Molloy's experiencing (rather than narrating) self. It must be said, though, that Molloy's extended cognitive system fails to help him to reach a satisfactory solution, which indicates that, just like Cartesianism, one should take cognitive extension in Beckett's work with a pinch of salt.

Molloy's attention to detail in dealing with his seemingly insurmountable task is reflected in the passage's genesis, as the second French notebook contains a number of diagrams and calculations of the whole process performed by Beckett himself (O'Reilly, Van Hulle and Verhulst, 2017, 212–14).[44] As mentioned in the Introduction, writing is a prime example of extended cognitive activity, and material objects such as pen and paper are indispensable for Beckett's own process of literary creation. In this example, both the author and the character display their extended minds, on different planes but nonetheless for similar purposes.

The nexus between the extended writing and fictional mind also manifests itself in Beckett's treatment of intertexuality in *Molloy*. As Knowlson observes, *Molloy* inaugurated Beckett's 'poetics of ignorance', as he denounced 'the Joycean principle that knowing more was a way of creatively understanding the world and controlling it' and the use of 'quotations and learned allusions to build up intellectually complex patterns of ideas and images' (1996, 353). Once again, this entrenched idea, although perfectly legitimate as a general comment, could benefit from revision from an extended cognitive vantage point.[45]

In literary studies, Dirk Van Hulle has suggested that the close relationship between the author's neural brain and their library, often in the form of marginalia or reading notes, 'is not just an illustration of . . . the "extended mind" (the writer's mind), but . . . also served as a model for many modernists' methods of evoking the workings of fictional minds (the characters' minds)' (2018, 68). He backs up his argument with examples from Joyce, Flann O'Brien, and Beckett (2014a, 151–82). A good illustration of Van Hulle's thesis is the following passage from *Molloy*, in which the narrator, while musing on his past and his idea of freedom, says the following:

---

[44] See *BDMP4*, www.beckettarchive.org/molloy/about/catalogue

[45] According to the principles of extended cognition, any encyclopaedic knowledge can considered external, even if it has been (partially) interiorised. Following the parity principle (Clark and Chalmers, 2010), it matters little where exactly that knowledge is 'located'. As long as is it *derived* (i.e., acquired from external sources), then the content of the human long-term memory is functionally similar to the content stored externally.

> I who had loved the image of old Geulincx, dead young, who left me free, on
> the black boat of Ulysses, to crawl towards the East, along the deck. That is
> a great measure of freedom, for him who has not the pioneering spirit. And
> from the poop, poring upon the wave, a sadly rejoicing slave, I follow with
> my eyes the proud and futile wake. Which, as it bears me from no fatherland
> away, bears me onwards to no shipwreck. (Beckett, 2009b, 50)

The image Molloy is conjuring up here certainly answers Knowlson's descrip-
tions of 'quotations and learned allusions' that Beckett supposedly left behind at
the time of writing *Molloy*, so whatever Beckett's intentions were at the time,
this passage can hardly be considered an exercise in ignorance. On the contrary,
it is a good example of Beckett's encyclopaedic erudition and his skill in
amalgamating several sources (in this case, Homer, Dante, Geulincx, and
possibly Joyce) in one elaborate and dense image.[46] The fact that Molloy,
who continuously underscores his ignorance, resorts to such a complex allusion
is at the very least unexpected, especially considering that *Molloy* supposedly
marks Beckett's departure from the Joycean *modus operandi* towards a poetics
of ignorance.[47]

The reason for this apparent contradiction between the self-professed poetics
of ignorance and the clear, if subtle, intertextual references might be the author's
(and the character's) 'extended mind'. As Van Hulle has suggested, due to the
modernist writers' comprehensive erudition, the acquired knowledge is so
entrenched in their own extended minds that it becomes instrumental in the
evocations of modernist *fictional* minds (2014a). Without disputing the fact that
the 'poetics of ignorance' was something Beckett earnestly aspired to, it seems
that he could not easily shed a vast body of literary and philosophical texts
stored in his extended mind, and this is reflected in Molloy's elaborate reference, creating another crossover between the author's and the character's
extended cognitive systems.

More important than this partial and occasional conflation of the character
and the writer is the more pronounced and deliberate conflation of the character
and the narrator that is palpable in *Molloy*. A consequence of the switch to the
first-person narration, this process is the first clear sign of the erosion of
Cartesian subject/object relations – the erosion that will continue to dominate
Beckett's prose for the rest of his writing career. Increasingly foregrounding
discourse over story, this new narrative strategy is a move from what H. Porter

---

[46] For a detailed analysis of the Geulincx passage in *Molloy*, see Tucker, 2012, 118–23.
[47] As David Tucker also notes (2012, 124), Geulincx returns, albeit in a more veiled form, in *The
Unnamable* – the work that belongs in Beckett's later period and as such should be even more
'purged' of learned intertextual allusions: 'The galley-man, bound for the Pillars of Hercules,
who drops his sweep under cover of night and crawls between the thwarts, towards the rising sun,
unseen by the guard, praying for storm' (Beckett, 2010d, 50).

Abbott calls 'aboutness' to 'isness', or from traditional narrative *representation* to narrative *enactment*.[48] As O'Reilly, Van Hulle, and Verhulst rightly note, '*Molloy* can be read as a demonstration or performance of [Beckett's] aesthetic vision. What is explained in *Dream of Fair to Middling Women* is enacted in *Molloy*' (2017, 225). This enactment is reflected upon by Molloy in his musings on the performative nature of language (Katz, 1999, 157–8):

> And then sometimes there arose within me, confusedly, a kind of *conscious-ness*, which I expressed by saying, I said, etc., or, Don't do it Molloy, or, Is that your mother's name? said the sergeant, I quote from memory. Or which I express without sinking to the level of oratio recta, but by means of other figures quite as deceitful, as for example, It seemed to me that, etc., or, I had the impression that, etc., for it seemed to me nothing at all, and I had no impression of any kind, but simply somewhere something had changed, so that I too had to change, or the world had to change, in order for nothing to be changed. And it was these little *adjustments*, as between Galileo's vessels, that I can only express by saying, I feared that, or, I hoped that, or, Is this your mother's name, said the sergeant, for example, and that I might doubtless have expressed otherwise and better, if I had gone to the trouble. And so I shall perhaps some day when I have less horror of trouble than today. But I think not. (Beckett, 2009b, 89–90; emphasis added)

In the above passage, Molloy conveys 'the sense of language, and even con-sciousness, as response and manoeuvre, or as Beckett calls it, "adjustment" – adjustment mobilized in the interest of stasis and preservation' (Katz, 1999, 158). It is indeed 'striking . . . that *language* is the name given to this sort of adjustment, be it internal or external. This implies, of course, a need to maintain a perspective on language as performative, on speaking not as a means of expression but as an act which produces effects on people and results in the "world"' (158–9).

Two points are of importance here. First of all, the way Daniel Katz assigns language a clearly action-oriented and performative role echoes Andy Clark's idea of language as an external tool that does not represent action but constitutes it (1997). Put another way, what Molloy seems to say is that by uttering those

---

[48] Abbott used the terms 'aboutness' and 'isness' in order to demonstrate the difference between representational and non-representational narratives: referring to Brian Richardson's anti-mimetic concept of unnatural narration (2006), he observes that 'much of twentieth-century experimental literature and film has not only abandoned traditional conventions of representation but representation altogether', creating 'texts that, in part or in whole, have relocated the intention of the art to what it does to the mind of the reader or viewer: from what art is *about* to what it cognitively *is*' (2013, 82). He specifically mentions Beckett's lines from 'Dante . . . Bruno. Vico.. Joyce' on Joyce's 'Work in Progress' ('His writing is not about something, it is that something itself') as an example of the modernist (and postmodernist) commitment to *isness* (92).

little phrases that he mentions, he was not *expressing* some inner conscious states, but actually *acting* on the world in order to achieve his purpose of maintaining the equilibrium between change and stasis.[49]

Also significant is the way Molloy labels his performative language – he actually refers to it as 'a kind of consciousness'. As Katz perceptively observes,

> [t]his gives us in all its radicality a conception of consciousness and interior monologue as performative. The passage is explicit: 'I feared' and 'I hoped' are not expressions of Molloy's anxiety at his realization that adjustment is necessary – *they are the adjustments themselves.* ... We have here a formulation of consciousness not as 'expressed' but rather as expression, and 'expression' not as mimesis but as performative. (1999, 158–9)

Just like in the case of language, consciousness is described here as an act rather than a representation of an act, an act that results in a different state of affairs in the world, and Katz's clever pun on Beckett's famous dictum in 'Dante ... Bruno. Vico.. Joyce' points at Beckett's attempts to reconcile his critical views with his own texts. The concept of consciousness as a performative act is arguably even more radical than Mark Rowlands' postcognitivist account of consciousness as an extended revealing activity,[50] as the former assigns consciousness a more active role. Either way, both approaches lead to 'the consideration of consciousness and concomitantly language as ... geared not toward representation, expression, or even formulation of attitudes, ideas, or mental conditions, but rather toward production and constitution of these conditions' (Katz, 1999, 159). It is remarkable that the scholar of a clearly poststructuralist persuasion unwittingly corroborates the postcognitivist interpretation of Molloy's cognitive activity.

In order to avoid terminological confusion, it is important to bear in mind that, despite the same root and similar meaning, literary *enactment* and cognitive *enaction* are two different concepts. In Beckett's case, although his later works enact the mind and the world instead of re-presenting them (thus deploying a more mimetic rather than diegetic narrative strategy), this does not necessarily entail an enactivist cognitive paradigm. For instance, as we shall see next, *Malone Dies* can be considered an enactment of the creative writing process that is grounded in an

---

[49] Language as an external component of an extended cognitive system will return in our discussion of Beckett's late works at the end of this section.

[50] Whereas Clark and Chalmers claim that conscious processes are by definition internal, Rowlands advances its extended nature by equating phenomenal consciousness (i.e., subjective experience or the 'what-it-is-likeness' of such experience; Chalmers, 1996, 28) with intentionality (i.e., the idea that mental states are always about something and thus directed towards the objects they refer to). Considering that phenomenal consciousness, which for Rowlands is synonymous with intentionality, serves to make connections between the world and our representations of that world (not unlike the link between a real object and its linguistic referent), it is always intentionally directed towards the world, and therefore by definition straddles both the external and internal components of cognition (Rowlands, 2015).

extended (rather than *enactive*) cognitive relationship between Malone and his writing tools. Likewise, some examples of literary enactment will pertain to exclusively internal forms of cognition, as *Molloy*'s long interior monologues testify. However, what both concepts do have in common is that they both entail a breakdown of Cartesian dualist subject/object relations: whereas literary enactment departs from the representational model of *narration*, enactivism dispenses with the representational model of the *mind* and suggests that cognition continuously shapes and is shaped by the environment it operates in.

Malone Dies *(1951)*

The erosion of the Cartesian subject/object relationship of representation continues in *Malone Dies*, which was written shortly after *Molloy*. Remarkably, though, the opening pages of the sequel suggest precisely the opposite: what we get is a narrator who announces from the very start that he is going to tell stories to pass the time, thus diverting the reader's attention from his own person to those invented by him. Unlike his predecessors (i.e., Molloy and Moran), he appears to have no commissioning agency above him to whom he would hand over the text, and he explicitly states that those stories are for himself only. What is also surprising is that he seems to have a plan ('my time-table' or 'programme', as he calls it) for his narrative endeavour:

> I think I shall be able to tell myself four stories, each one on a different theme. One about a man, another about a woman, a third about a thing and finally one about an animal, a bird probably. I think that is everything. . . . then I shall speak of the things that remain in my possession . . . It will be a kind of inventory. (Beckett, 2010b, 5)

After some musing on the number and the order of his stories, he arrives at the following conclusion: 'Present state, three stories, inventory, there. An occasional interlude is to be feared. A full programme. I shall not deviate from it any further than I must' (6). Rather than enactment, signalled in *Molloy*, what the reader is ostensibly promised is some good old-fashioned representations churned out by the isolated Cartesian mind of a third-person narrator.

However, and not entirely unexpectedly, the Cartesian image conjured at the outset of the novel quickly unravels to reveal a much more consistent case of cognitive extension than in *Molloy*. Despite the presence of the stories (though not quite those announced in Malone's 'programme'), the whole novel can be seen as one long meta-comment on itself – or, put another way, an enactment of the painstaking and at times excruciating process of creative writing.

Unlike his predecessors, Malone's interaction with the world is limited because his partial paralysis severely restricts his action possibilities: as

Malone himself admits, 'if I had the use of my body I would throw it out of the window' (Beckett, 2010b, 45). Instead, all he can do is passively wait for his life to expire. On top of that, Malone's physical disability prevents him from garnering first-hand knowledge of his environment. Deprived of the possibility to leave his room or even to move around it, Malone can only make conjectures about his whereabouts, and the only phenomenological experiences he can rely on are the sounds he hears and the light he sees coming through the window.

Restricted knowledge and severely limited manipulation of his environment also affect Malone's thought processes: unable to interact with others or the world, he tells himself stories and writes them down to pass the time. The writing component is significant: using the few affordances he still has at his disposal, Malone resorts to writing as an extended cognitive activity, thus maximising his interaction with his environment, however limited the latter may be.[51] Malone is keenly aware of the advantages of writing versus oral storytelling:

> I did not want to write, but I had to resign myself to it in the end. It is in order to know where I have got to go, where he [Sapo] has got to. At first I did not write, I just said the thing. Then I forgot what I said. A minimum of memory is indispensable, if one is to live really. Take his family, for example, I really know practically nothing about his family any more. But that does not worry me, there is a record of it somewhere. (Beckett, 2010b, 33)

So far, the use of external cognitive artefacts (such as the pencil and the exercise book)[52] seems to have a purely mnemonic function, but Malone's parallel to recording his own tale in the present state discredits the idea of an extended mind solely as a memory aid, as he continues:

> But as far as I myself am concerned the same necessity does not arise, or does it? And yet I write about myself with the same pencil and in the same exercise-book as about him. It is because it is no longer I, ... but another whose life is just beginning. It is right that he too should have his little chronicle, his memories, his reason, and to be able to recognize the good in the bad, the bad in the worst, and so grow gently old all down the unchanging

---

[51] In his discussion of Malone's physical disability, Paul Sheehan remarks that Malone 'is unable to manipulate and coordinate his body, as he readily admits' (2017, 143). Though this may be true for most of his physical activity, Malone – and this is crucial – does have the use of his hands and upper body, at least in sufficient measure to be able to execute a writing task. Without the body as a coordinating agency between 'thought and action' (Sheehan, 2017, 143), no extended or enactive cognitive system is possible.

[52] In his book *Things that Make Us Smart* (1993), Donald A. Norman defines cognitive artefacts as 'those artificial devices that maintain, display, or operate upon information in order to serve a representational function and that affect human cognitive performance' (17), whereby 'artificial' stands for 'man-made'.

days and die one day like any other day, only shorter. That is my excuse. (Beckett, 2010b, 33–4)

It is clear from this passage that Malone's extended writing activity transcends the purely mnemonic purpose and produces a different, narrative version of himself: it seems that 'writing ... allows [Malone] to off-load his "self"' (Sheehan, 2017, 143). As Sheehan explains: 'Malone is only too eager to be rid of the burdensome construct that is the "self". And the most effective way of doing this, he finds, is through language – written language, however, not spoken' (143).[53]

The intense interaction between Malone and his writing tools raises the issue of the mind/world boundary, for which Clark and Chalmers' fundamental question 'Where does the mind stop and the rest of the world begin?' (2010, 27) serves as a good starting point. In this connection, two objects in Malone's possession are particularly interesting: Malone's stick as an extension of his body, and his exercise book as an extension of his mind.

In his study of Beckett's prosthetic bodies, Yoshiki Tajiri invokes Malone's stick from a psychoanalytical rather than philosophical angle: 'Just like Molloy's bicycle and crutches, the stick is more than an ordinary prosthesis. Apart from his writing, which he performs with his pencil and exercise-book, most of Malone's physical action rests on this stick. ... [T]he stick seems to be incorporated into the body and function like a sentient hand – a better hand, actually' (2007, 44–5). As a critique of the Cartesian dualist model, Tajiri sees 'the prosthetic body as a locus of interaction between the inside and the outside' (56).[54] This echoes Merleau-Ponty's well-known example of a blind person's cane (Merleau-Ponty, 1962, 139–41), in which he also questions the body/world boundary, this time from a phenomenological but equally anti-Cartesian angle.

A possible instance of Beckett's own critique on Cartesianism (or, in any case, of representationalism in general) is the episode in which Malone loses his stick:

I have lost my stick, That is the outstanding event of the day, for it is day again. ... It is a disaster. I suppose the wisest thing now is to live it over again, meditate upon it and be edified. It is thus that man distinguishes himself from the ape and rises, from discovery to discovery, ever higher, towards the light. Now that I have lost my stick I realize what it is I have lost and all it meant to me. And thence ascend, painfully, to an understanding of the Stick, shorn of all its accidents, such as I had never dreamt of. What a broadening of the mind. (Beckett, 2010b, 82–3)

---

[53] For a detailed postcognitivist account of writing as an extended cognitive activity, see Menary, 2007.

[54] The psychoanalytic approach in Beckett studies is a large domain in its own right, and I could not possibly do it justice within the tight format of the present study. Tajiri's reading is primarily meant to serve as an illustration that anti-Cartesianism is not a solely postcognitivist affair.

It is hard not to spot the irony in Malone's words as he sketches the traditional representationalist account of cognition and the place it ostensibly occupies in our value system, even though there is no question here of any alternative suggestions. That said, the Cartesian system is never far away and comes to the fore in Malone's musings about his abode: 'You may say it is all in my head, and indeed sometimes it seems to me I am in a head and that these eight, no, six, these six planes that enclose me are of solid bone. But thence to conclude the head is mine, no, never' (48). Although the last sentence somehow qualifies the otherwise perfectly dualist image of the hermetically isolated mind, it is easy to see why early Beckett scholars had no problem finding textual evidence to corroborate their Cartesian bias. Even Paul Sheehan, who considers *Malone Dies* from a postcognitivist perspective, reads this passage as an indication that 'there is no mind to extend – or not a mind of which Malone can claim ownership' (2017, 143). However, if we consider *Malone Dies* to be about the writing process, then it is hard to deny that Malone's writing mind does extend into his world (however reduced it may be) during the act of writing, as the following example will demonstrate.

What the stick is to Malone's body, the exercise book is to Malone's mind. Bearing in mind that the writing process is an instance of an extended mind, Malone's use of and attachment to his exercise book deserve closer scrutiny. From the start, he distinguishes between all other items among his possessions (including the pencil) and the exercise book – '[t]he exercise-book ... seems almost to be part of him' (Sheehan, 2017, 144):

> My exercise-book, I don't see it, but I feel it in my left hand, I don't know where it comes from, I didn't have it when I came here, but I feel it's mine. That's the style, as if I were sweet and seventy. In this case the bed would be mine too, and the little table, the dish, the pots, the cupboard, the blankets. No, nothing of all that is mine. But the exercise-book is mine, I can't explain. (Beckett, 2010b, 75)

On another occasion Malone calls it 'human' (100) and admits that it is 'his life' (104). The exercise book is also described in great detail:

> It is ruled in squares. The first pages are covered with ciphers and other symbols and diagrams, with here and there a brief phrase. Calculations, I reckon. They seem to stop suddenly, prematurely at all events. As though discouraged. Perhaps it is astronomy, or astrology. I did not look closely. I drew a line, no, I did not even draw a line, and I wrote, Soon I shall be quite dead at last, and so on, without even going on to the next page, which was blank. (Beckett, 2010b, 35)

Remarkably, this description bears close resemblance to Beckett's own extended vehicle of thought, namely the very notebook in which he began writing *Malone Dies*. The French original, *Malone meurt*, 'was begun at the back of the fifth notebook containing the manuscript of Beckett's novel *Watt*' (Carlton Lake, qtd in Van Hulle and Verhulst, 2017, 36). Both the fictional and original notebooks are ruled in squares, and 'the "first pages" that Malone alludes to … do correspond to the last few pages of the *Watt* manuscript in Beckett's notebook. There are some calculations on 46 v and Beckett made three circular drawings on 48 v that resemble planets and celestial bodies orbiting them' (Van Hulle and Verhulst, 2017, 37). In his discussion of Malone's description of his exercise book, Peter Boxall likewise finds it 'difficult to resist the thought that Malone is describing in part the notebook which contains the opening of Beckett's draft of *Malone meurt*, and which interrupts the manuscript of *Watt*, where that earlier novel had stopped, "as though discouraged"' (Beckett, 2010b, xii).[55] Just like in the case of Molloy's sucking stones episode, the example of Malone's exercise book points to an extended cognitive system on both the level of composition and of narration. To use Bernini's term, both Beckett and Malone qualify as 'extended-mind workers' in their creative writing activity.

Staying on the level of narration, the exercise book becomes the scene of the ultimate conflation of Malone the narrator with his story at the novel's end. The grand finale, both of Malone's tale and (ostensibly) his own life, takes the form of Lemuel's killing spree:

> Lemuel made Macmann and the two others get into the boat and got into it himself. Then they set out, all six, from the shore.
>
> Gurgles of outflow.
>
> This tangle of grey bodies is they. Silent, dim, perhaps clinging to one another, their heads buried in their cloaks, they lie together in a heap, in the night. They are far out in the bay. Lemuel has shipped his oars, the oars trail in the water. The night is strewn with absurd
>
> absurd lights, the stars, the beacons, the buoys, the lights of earth and in the hills the faint fires of the blazing gorse. *Macmann, my last, my possessions, I remember*, he is there too, perhaps he sleeps. Lemuel
>
> Lemuel is in charge, he raises his hatchet on which the blood will never dry, but not to hit anyone, he will not hit anyone, he will not hit anyone any more, he will not touch anyone any more, either with it or with it or with it or with or
>
> or with it or *with his hammer or with his stick or with his fist or in thought in dream* I mean never he will never

---

[55] In their genetic study of the novel, Van Hulle and Verhulst provide more examples of Beckett's writing process seemingly overlapping with Malone's (2017, 25–6).

> or *with his pencil or with his stick or*
> or light light I mean
> never there he will never
> never anything
> there
> any more (Beckett, 2010b, 118–19; emphasis added)

Apart from the actual text (containing multiple repetitions), the page's layout, with the abundance of white space and interrupted sentences, enacts the moribund narrator's increasingly failing attempts to finish his tale.[56] The words in italics signal the key moments in which the narrator merges with his story, thus eroding the traditional novelistic subject/object relation almost beyond the point of recognition. As a consequence, the outside/inside dichotomy dissipates, obscuring the neat spatiotemporal properties inherent to any story. The end of *Malone Dies* drives the last nail into the coffin in which Beckett's earlier prose style lies buried, the style that was systematically butchered throughout the novel, with Lemuel's hatchet serving as an appropriate metaphor in this case.

Discourse: Enactivism

The end of *Malone Dies* is a poignant illustration of a continuous shift in Beckett's narrative strategy from representation to enactment. The narrator, who is no longer capable of detached observation of a pre-given fictional world, merges with that world and therefore relinquishes the dominance of the Cartesian subject over the object of his cognitive activity. The shift to narrative enactment also foregrounds the discourse element at the expense of the story: since there is no story to re-present, the narrating agency itself and its relationship to the narrative become the centre of attention.

This development resonates with Beckett's own critical views, famously expressed in his correspondence with Georges Duthuit in the late 1940s. In a letter dated 9 March 1949, written – crucially – between *Malone Dies* and *The Unnamable*, Beckett discusses the notion of relation, in different senses of the word: both 'the primary form, that between the artist and the outside world', and relations within the artist himself (*LSB II*, 138). The key question Beckett poses is this: 'Can one conceive of expression in the *absence* of relations of whatever kind, whether those between "I" and "non-I" or those within the former?' (139; emphasis added). What Beckett calls for is the rejection of 'the state of being in

---

[56] In a letter to Mania Péron regarding the ending of the novel, Beckett admitted struggling with it even at the proofs stage. The delicate balance he endeavoured to maintain was that '[the end] had to work *actively*, but not too much, not to the point of extinguishing the effort to end' (*LSB II*, 303; also qtd in Van Hulle and Verhulst, 2017, 253; emphasis added). The 'active' nature of the ending was thus very much intended by the author.

a relation as such, the state of being in front of' (140). Using the example of Bram van Velde as the painter who got it right, Beckett admonishes others to be 'brave enough ... to grasp that the break with the outside world entails the break with the inside world, [because] there are no replacement relations for naïve relations, [and] *what are called outside and inside are one and the same*' (140, emphasis added). At the end of the letter Beckett makes a crucial statement about his own work: 'I am no longer capable of writing *about*' (141), meaning that he, like Bram van Velde in painting, does not wish to place himself in a representational subject/object relation to his art, to be 'in front of' anything.

The Unnamable *(1953)*

According to Dirk Van Hulle, '[the Duthuit letter] is the background against which Beckett is writing *L'Innommable*, in which the first-person narrator thematises this interplay between inside and outside' (2014a, 204). In this sense, '*L'Innommable* can be read as an attempt (not necessarily successful) to find an alternative model of the mind' (190). By 'alternative' Van Hulle means an 'alternative to the Cartesian mind-body split', and the manner in which Beckett supposedly achieved this is by 'a mingling of "inside" and "outside"' (203): 'One could even argue that *L'Innommable* prefigures the more recent cognitive paradigm of 'enaction', which sees the mind, not as something that takes place exclusively inside a head, but as something that consists of a constant interaction between the brain and the environment' (203). The challenge that the novel presents for a postcognitivist account of cognition is that its storyworld – the environment for the fictional mind to interact with – is stripped of nearly all materiality, thus depriving us of the very possibility of constructing an extended cognitive system involving objects, such as that of Malone and his exercise book or Molloy and his sucking stones. At the same time, immateriality is not tantamount to interiority, and ephemeral elements such as sound, light, and voices are just as much part of the environment as are tangible objects. Moreover, due to their 'ineffable' nature, the voices in *The Unnamable* are difficult to place with any degree of certainty either inside (the Unnamable's brain) or outside (coming from elsewhere and invading it). This persistent ambiguity only adds to the erosion of the Cartesian mind/world dichotomy in the novel and facilitates the merging of inside and outside, which calls for an *enactive* rather than *extended* postcognitivist paradigm in the analysis of the narrator's cognitive activity.

The central issue in our discussion will be – predictably – the 'question of voices', or, to be more precise, the source and identity of the narrating voice. This voice will be considered from a postcognitivist angle to see how it oscillates between the Cartesian 'cogito' and an enactive cognitive system that does away with dualist boundaries. From the outset, *The Unnamable*'s narrator struggles to find his voice in order to carry on the storytelling after the demise of his predecessor, Malone. He openly renounces his narrative responsibility and places himself on the receiving end of information:

> It seems to me it was none of my doing. We won't go into this now. I can see them still, my delegates. The things they have told me! About men, the light of day. I refused to believe them. But some of it has stuck. But when, through what channels did I communicate with these gentlemen? . . . When did all this nonsense stop? And has it stopped? . . . There were four or five of them at me, they called that presenting their report. (Beckett, 2010d, 8)

This way, the Unnamable's 'delegates', hitherto known as 'a few puppets' (2) or mere avatars of the narrator, turn out to be narrators themselves (by means of 'presenting their report'). As Daniel Katz notes,

> the voice talks of its 'delegates' not as characters of its own creation but almost as the opposite; rather than that which represents the voice, that *through which* the voice speaks, here the 'delegates' are that which speaks *to* the voice, that which gives the voice what it has to speak. . . . The 'voice' cannot be read as presenting an essence in its pure, interiorized form, as it only exists in the space of its own exteriority. (1999, 104)

Approaching the issue from a poststructuralist perspective, Katz points to the illusory nature of representations, as it is completely unclear in this case who is representing whom. The reason for this is the apparent impossibility of any pre-given knowledge or meaning, the thesis that underlies enactive approaches to cognition.

In another poststructuralist text, Yoshiki Tajiri (2007) discusses the notion of 'the prosthetic voice' from a clearly Derridean perspective, using the latter's concept of 'différance' as a departure point. As we saw earlier, the unnamable narrator seems to suggest that the voice that emanates from him is not his at all, but comes from elsewhere:

> The voice that speaks, . . . [i]t issues from me, it fills me, it clamours against my walls, it is not mine, I can't stop it, I can't prevent it, from tearing me, racking me, assailing me. It is not mine, I have none, I have no voice and must speak, that is all I know, it's round that I must revolve, of that I must speak, with this voice that is not mine, but can only be mine . . . (Beckett 2010d, 17–18)
>
> They've blown me up with their voices, like a balloon, and even as I collapse it's them I hear. Who, them? (37)
>
> Is there a single word of mine in all I say? No, I have no voice, in this matter I have none. . . . But I don't say anything, I don't know anything, these voices

are not mine, nor these thoughts, but the voices and thoughts of the devils who beset me. (61)

Just as it was with Katz's approach, Tajiri's poststructuralist concept of the prosthetic voice bears some interesting similarities to the postcognitivist discourse: for instance, he remarks on the fact that the Unnamable first hears the voice and then speaks (whereas the opposite order would be more natural, assuming the voice is his). According to Tajiri, 'if the originary moment is that of hearing, it means that there is no originary moment at all, because hearing is necessarily a secondary act, and also because with the total breakdown of subjectivity in *The Unnamable*, the hearing "I" will be no more originary or self-sufficient than the speaking "I"' (2007, 141).

Tajiri's conclusion on the impossibility of originary knowledge is strikingly similar to Hutto and Myin's radical enactivist concept of the content-free basic mind (2013).[57] The content-free basic mind – also known as the extensive mind (i.e., the mind engaged in familiar activity such as catching a ball) – does not store any mental representations at all and interacts with its environment in an unmediated, non-representational way. Applied to the novel, the lack of any intrinsic mental knowledge shows in the embodied way in which the Unnamable gains information about his present state:

> I, of whom I know nothing, I know my eyes are open, because of the tears that pour from them unceasingly. I know I am seated, my hands on my knees, because of the pressure against my rump, against the soles of my feet, against the palms of my hands, against my knees. (Beckett, 2010d, 14–15)[58]

For more complex cognitive activity, such as anything involving language, basic minds transform into 'contentful scaffolded minds' (Hutto and Myin, 2013, 152). However, that content is never non-derived but consists in external 'linguistic symbols and forms of cognition that feature in . . . shared, scaffolded practices' (151–2), the mind absorbing the knowledge available in the environment, with the learning process facilitated by the stability of generally accepted sociocultural and linguistic conventions. The image that the Unnamable conjures of himself being filled with other voices serves as a powerful illustration of Hutto and Myin's concept.

The picture sketched above of the Unnamable's embodied/enactive cognitive activity may lead to the conclusion that Cartesian dualism has been finally

---

[57] Mark Rowlands, another proponent of postcognitivism, has also suggested the impossibility of non-derived, intrinsic mental content, claiming that content always comes from beyond the brain (2015).

[58] As we saw in our discussion of Maude's embodied approach to Beckett's work, a very similar example can be found in *Company*, where the hearer's awareness of his position derives directly from his bodily sensations.

vanquished and banished from Beckett's oeuvre. This is certainly not the case: Cartesian imagery is still present in the text as well as in the manuscript of *The Unnamable*. The most illustrative one (in the literal sense of the word) is a detailed drawing in the second French notebook of a humanlike creature with a homunculus inside his large head (for details, see *BDMP2*[59] and Van Hulle and Weller, 2014, 117–19; 153–5). The notion of the homunculus, already encountered in *Malone Dies*, assumes several guises in the drafts of *L'Innommable*: 'the "I" first describes his predecessors as "remplaçants", and then this word is replaced by "homuncules": "derrière mes remplaçants homuncules, je n'ai pas toujours été triste" (FN1, 16 v)' (Van Hulle and Weller, 2014, 117); the word Beckett employed in the English translations was 'mannikins').[60] Further down in the same notebook, the word reappears with regard to Worm, when the latter is described as 'pseudo-homuncule' (*BDMP2*, FN1, 66 v; omitted in the published version). In the second French notebook, the elaborate drawing of the little man inside the head of a larger anthropomorphic creature (*BDMP2*, FN2, 21 r) is followed a few pages later by the Unnamable's suggestion that he might be inside a head (*BDMP2*, FN2, 24 v; Van Hulle and Weller, 2014, 153).[61] In the published English version, we find the following Cartesian (if slightly unorthodox) rendering of the Unnamable's mind: 'I on whom all dangles, better still, about whom, much better, all turns, dizzily, yes yes, don't protest, all spins, it's a head, I'm in a head, what an illumination, sssst, pissed on out of hand' (Beckett, 2010d, 88). However, the ironic tone of the sentence immediately undermines the solidity of the Cartesian edifice constructed, albeit hesitantly, in the rest of the passage.

This hesitation, this split between the two systems – on the one hand, severely disrupting but not quite abandoning the Cartesian model, and on the other, groping as though in the dark for an alternative that is beckoning and yet still out of reach – is expressed with great precision in the well-known (and much-discussed) tympanum metaphor:

> I'll have said it inside me, then in the same breath outside me, perhaps that's what I feel, an outside and an inside and me in the middle, perhaps that's what I am, the thing that divides the world in two, on the one side the outside, on the other the inside, that can be as thin as foil, *I'm neither one side nor the other,*

---

[59] www.beckettarchive.org/catalogues/innommable/catalogue
[60] Van Hulle and Weller note (2014, 117) that Beckett makes a small drawing of a homunculus a few pages later (19v). Though the idea of a homunculus may have come from Beckett's reading of *Faust* in 1936 (117), it is vital for the Cartesian model of the mind (119), as it not only explains the mind/world dualism, but also exposes one of its most fundamental flaws, namely the infinite regress of the homunculus model (119).
[61] The phrase 'je suis dans une tête' was already mentioned in the first French notebook on 72v (Van Hulle and Weller, 2014, 153).

> *I'm in the middle, I'm the partition, I've two surfaces and no thickness,*
> *perhaps that's what I feel, myself vibrating, I'm the tympanum, on the one*
> hand the mind, *on the other the world, I don't belong to either,* it's not to me
> they're talking, it's not of me they're talking, no, that's not it … (Beckett,
> 2010d, 100; emphasis added)

This passage reiterates the problematic relationship between the inside and the
outside that Beckett expounded on in his letter to Duthuit. Interestingly, the
French original and the earlier English versions contain the word 'le crâne'/
'the skull' instead of 'the mind' (Van Hulle, 2014a, 205), but the emendation
in the English text from 'the skull' to 'the mind' makes the formulation even
more Cartesian (after all, the skull is part of the body and thus belongs to the
material world). In any case,

> [w]hat the narrator of *The Unnamable* describes is not a 'skullscape' … the
> landscape of the inside of a skull; instead, it emphasizes the *interaction* or
> vibration between neural and environmental elements, which is a continuous
> process. Hence the word 'on', which becomes increasingly prominent in
> Beckett's works, from the last line of *The Unnamable* … to the first line of
> *Worstward Ho*. (Van Hulle, 2014a, 205)

The explicit and unequivocal placing of the Unnamable exactly on the dualist
mind/world boundary underscores the transitional nature of the text. Towards
the end, the Cartesian doctrine seems to regain the ostensibly lost momentum:

> it's an image, those are words, it's a body, it's not I, I knew it wouldn't be I,
> I'm not outside, I'm inside, I'm in something, I'm shut up, the silence is
> outside, outside, inside, there is nothing but here, and the silence outside,
> nothing but this voice and the silence all round, no need of walls, yes, we must
> have walls, I need walls, good and thick, I need a prison, I was right, for me
> alone, I'll go there now, I'll put me in it, I'm there already …
>
>   The place, I'll make it all the same, I'll make it in my head, I'll draw it out
> of my memory, I'll gather it all about me, I'll make myself a head, I'll make
> myself a memory … (Beckett, 2010d, 130–1)

The above passages suggest a return to a confined space, to being inside rather
than outside, and the head seems to be once again celebrated as 'the seat of all'
(Beckett 2009a, 87). However, the joy of finally registering the hitherto elusive
Beckettian 'inward turn' again appears premature, as the second passage continues thus:

> The place, I'll make it all the same, I'll make it in my head, I'll draw it out of
> my memory, I'll gather it all about me, I'll make myself a head, I'll make
> myself a memory, *I have only to listen, the voice will tell me everything, tell it*
> *to me again, everything I need, in dribs and drabs, breathless* … (Beckett,
> 2010d, 131; emphasis added)

Just as you thought that the interior mind (in the head) is about to take charge, it turns out that we have come back to the elusive question of voices. Although their origin remains a mystery, the text seems to suggest that they come from without rather than within: 'in *L'Innommable*, the stories ... issue forth *as if* from a single source, but the single "I" is quick to point out that they issue forth from other voices and that the "I" is actually "not I"' (Van Hulle, 2014b, 32). The presence of ostensibly external voices may not lead to a complete unravelling of the Cartesian representational model of the mind, but it surely deals it a considerable blow.

In the Trilogy as a whole, a clear evolution with regard to the question of voices can be discerned. Molloy is the only one who speaks unequivocally of 'a voice far away *inside* me' (Beckett 2009b, 89; emphasis added), leaving no doubt as to where the voice issues from. *Malone Dies* is more ambivalent, but 'may still suggest that the "streams of narrative" (Dennett, 1993, 418) issue forth "from one mouth, or one pencil or pen" (418)' (Van Hulle, 2014b, 32). *The Unnamable* leaves the providence and ownership of the voice hanging in the air, but the abiding impression is that they come from some unidentified *external* source. The question of the voice's origin will remain crucial and largely unresolved in Beckett's subsequent work, with *Company* being the text that probably best reflects the full degree of its complexity.[62]

The arguments and textual examples presented here point to an unravelling of the Cartesian mind and towards a system in which the dualist boundary no longer holds – namely, an enactive cognitive paradigm. As John Stewart notes, 'a living organism is not so much a "thing," but rather a process with the particular property of *engendering itself* indefinitely' (2010, 2). Moreover, the enactivist model of the mind contends that the organism's cognitive actions 'modify the environment and/or the relation of the organism to its environment, and hence modify in return the sensory input' (3). The unnamable narrator's enactive mind continuously draws on environmental inputs (voices and bodily sensations) in order to generate output (speech) that in turn, once uttered, becomes part of the environment, thus generating a seemingly endless feedback loop. In the end, it is quite impossible to pinpoint the borderline between the inside and the outside of the Unnamable's cognitive activity, because the creator is at the same time the creation, and vice versa.[63] Recalling the constituents of Di Paolo, Rohde, and De Jaegher's (2010) enactive cognitive system discussed briefly in the Introduction, what is invoked in *The Unnamable* qualifies as such

---

[62] For a discussion of *Company* as an enactive cognitive system, see Beloborodova 2018.

[63] As Tajiri remarks, '[the] "vice-existers" [as the Unnamable calls Basil/Mahood and Worm, as well as (possibly) the M-characters from Beckett's previous works] are necessary to "form" the narrator's self, although they are also alien to it' (2007, 140).

on all accounts: despite its continuous faltering and fumbling, the feedback loop between the cognising agent and the voices is autonomous and self-generating, ensuring that the Unnamable can go on against all odds. The system is also engaged in the process of sense-making, even though that avenue does not prove to be very successful. It is constantly (re-)emerging, in different guises (such as Mahood or Worm), and it is embodied both in a physical sense, through the Unnamable's decimated but still present body, and through a number of 'delegates', 'avatars', and 'vice-existers' from whom the torrent of voices seems to issue. Finally, the system draws on its prior experience in order to anticipate future developments, to which the repetitive structure of the Unnamable's verbal outpourings attests. At the end of the text, the autopoiesis is underscored by the Unnamable's last words: 'you must go on, I can't go on, I'll go on' (Beckett, 2010d, 134).

The ostensibly self-reliant and isolated interior Cartesian mind, initially present (if only to be parodied) in Beckett's early work, progressively unravels as his texts mature and eventually falls apart by the time the Trilogy has been finished. The Unnamable's plight is a convincing example of someone's repeated attempts to take an inward plunge in shallow waters, only to discover that they hit rock bottom straight away every time. For a large part of the text, the increasingly desperate cognising agent is trying to discover his identity but increasingly realises that he has none, consisting instead of incessant and inescapable inputs from without. No matter how hard he resists, he cannot help being filled by the voices he hears, so much so that they often pass for his, since he is the one doing the actual speaking. The enactive feedback loop runs full force and shows no signs of ceasing, despite the Unnamable's anguish, as the mind cannot stop functioning, much like the artist cannot stop expressing himself (even if there is nothing to express, as Beckett famously argued in his 'Three Dialogues'). If *Malone Dies* enacts the cognitive process of writing (or creative storytelling), then *The Unnamable* could be said to enact cognition in general – not just the need to create stories or express oneself, but the inability to stop thinking in language.

Though still rudimentary and shaky, the enactive cognitive system in *The Unnamable* nonetheless deals a serious blow to the ubiquitous all-internal Cartesian mind, isolated and in possession of pre-given (representation-based) world knowledge. That said, it is hard to ignore the signs that Descartes' ghost still haunts the text, such as the doodle of (presumably) the homunculus in the second French notebook, or the persistent thematisation of the inside/ outside dichotomy, most poignantly expressed by the tympanum metaphor. This makes *The Unnamable* a transitional work in more ways than one: the move from story to discourse is almost but not quite complete (there are still stories in the text); the inside/outside opposition is lifted but still continuously foregrounded; the materiality of the storyworld is all but gone (as the Unnamable succinctly puts it, 'the days of sticks are over' (11)), yet the discourse is embodied through the Unnamable's own deformed physicality and the evocations of his 'avatars'. Besides, one cannot fail to notice that the Unnamable is extremely negative towards the environmental elements that constitute his cognition: he sees them as something intrusive and menacing, rather than parts of an ingenious survival strategy (as the enactive approach would suggest) or handy external scaffolding to engage with (as language is typically perceived from a postcognitivist perspective). Despite his attempts to purge himself of all extraneous influences, the Unnamable seems to lack any intrinsic knowledge of his own in order to go on, even though he is utterly frustrated about his impotence and dependence on environmental inputs that the voices constitute. In the works that will follow, this raging negativity will turn into cold-blooded violence in *How It Is* but will disappear completely in *Company*, giving way to melancholy and surrender.

Worstward Ho *(1983)*

At this point, our own narrative is going to take a giant leap forward, right to the very end of Beckett's writing life, to discuss *Worstward Ho* and 'what is the word'. The reason for the leap is twofold. On the practical side, the minigraph format of the present study does not allow for an exhaustive account of Beckett's prose, so the end result will inevitably be a selection. The more pertinent reason is that both *Worstward Ho* and 'what is the word' are, each in their own way, vivid illustrations of language as part of an extended cognitive system. Although featuring prominently in the above discussion of the Trilogy, it is in these two works that language as a means for the mind to extend into the world gains particular importance.

One of the most striking features of *Worstward Ho*, and one that catches the reader's eye from the very start, is its dynamic, action-oriented style. Enclosed in the opening and closing imperative ('on'), an echo from the Unnamable's last words, the fictional mind evoked in the text propels itself forward, and this incessant energy and determination, usually associated with productive activity, is paradoxically deployed in a deconstructive quest for the worst. If any externalism is to be traced in *Worstward Ho*, it will certainly be an active one.

That said, *Worstward Ho* also abounds in Cartesian imagery, and the very first paragraph states the Cartesian case quite clearly: 'Say a body. Where none. No mind. Where none. That at least. A place. Where none. For the body. To be in.

Move in. Out of. Back into. No. No out. No back. Only in. Stay in. On in. Still'. (Beckett, 2009a, 81) Throughout the text, the head (or skull) is referred to as 'Seat of all', 'Germ of all', and 'Scene and seer of all'. At the same time, the story is not as unequivocal as it seems, as Dirk Van Hulle's glimpse into the text's genesis reveals:

> In the first draft the 'inward turn' was much more explicit: 'The skull *within*. The *inward* staring eyes. Little to worsen there' (UoR MS 2602/1, 9 r; Beckett 1998, 177). By gradually changing this 'skull within' and the 'inward staring eyes' of the first version into 'the *so-said* seat and germ of all' of the published version (Beckett, 2009a, 90; emphasis added), Beckett 'decreated' or creatively undid the old models of the mind, and paved the way for a post-cognitivist approach. (2012, 287; emphasis added)

This postcognitivist approach entails the only means left at the exasperated narrator's disposal to fill the void of the storyworld, namely his use of language. Before turning again to the text for examples of the way the narrator's mind extends through language, a brief note on the status of language in postcogni-tivist theories of cognition will supply the necessary context.

Andy Clark, one of the champions of the extended mind thesis, sees language as the 'ultimate cognitive artefact' (1997). The main premise of Clark's discus-sion is that language is much more than a tool for communication; instead, language provides scaffolding for the brain to expand its capacity.[64] The American language philosopher Christopher Gauker goes even further, suggest-ing that language is 'not a tool for representing the world or expressing our thoughts but a tool for effecting changes in one's environment' (1990, 31, qtd in Clark 1997, 196). As Clark notes, 'Gauker sees the role of language as ... directly causal: as a way of getting things done' (196). Another interesting insight is Peter Carruthers' idea of *public thinking*, as he suggests that 'one does not *first* entertain a private thought and then write it down: rather, the thinking *is* the writing' (1996, 52, qtd in Clark, 1997, 197).[65] Building on Carruthers' argument, the narrator's speech in *Worstward Ho* could be seen as a good example of *public thinking* in literature, with its meanderings, interruptions, self-contradicting, and portmanteau words (incidentally, the idea is not entirely dissimilar to the modernist stream of consciousness or interior monologue techniques). Clark emphasises the external nature of language and sees it 'as an external artefact designed to *complement* rather than *transfigure* the basic

---

[64] As we saw in our discussion of *The Unnamable*, this is also what Hutto and Myin suggest in their radical enactivist 'extensive mind' theory (2013).

[65] This is reminiscent of our discussion of Molloy's performative language as a means of effecting changes or 'adjustments' in the world (see earlier).

processing profile we share with other animals [rather than] as a source of profound inner reprogramming' (200; emphasis added).

One of Clark's basic insights is that although 'it is natural to suppose that words are always rooted in the fertile soil of pre-existing thoughts, ... sometimes, at least, the influence seems to run in the other direction' (208). Clark invokes poetry as his example, referring to all manner of linguistic constraints that a poem requires, and the need for the poet to operate within those constraints. A distinctive feature of *Worstward Ho* is that despite these constraints, the language used by the narrator – the external tool at his disposal in order to conjure up his world and extend into it – is mostly violated, uprooted, and abused: 'So leastwards on. So long as dim still. Dim undimmed. Or dimmed to dimmer still. To dimmost dim. Leastmost in dimmost dim. Utmost dim. Leastmost in utmost dim. Unworsenable worst' (Beckett, 2009a, 95). This passage contains almost as many neologisms as extant words, not to mention the complete (and deliberate) disregard for syntax. Another example of the same is the very first sentence: 'On. Say on. Be said on. Somehow on. Till nohow on. Said nohow on' (81).

The fragmented sentences, the numerous grammatical violations, the abundance of interruptions and contradictions – all these linguistic anomalies serve to sketch an equally fragmented, confused, restless, and contradictory fictional mind. It is the mind's creative power that wields language at its own discretion and at the same time is wielded by it. At this point, one important caveat must be made: unlike Joyce, who worked his magic mostly on the so-called open-class members of the lexicon that can be replenished by neologisms, Beckett's 'late style' is marked by his 'attempt to create an art made largely out of the syntacticon,[66] while scarcely exploiting the dictionary – forming what Beckett calls "tattered syntaxes"' (Banfield, 2003, 17).[67] With regard to *Worstward Ho*, Ann Banfield also notes that 'the text strains to coin new members of nonproductive classes, as in the directional prepositional proforms ["Thenceless thitherless there"; "Whencesoever"; "Whithersoever"; "Worstward"] or the new preposition "atween" ... using the semi-productive English prefix "a-"' (22). The narrator's assault on the very core of language – its seemingly unshakeable syntax and the closed class of function words – testifies to a more profound cognitive coupling between the neural brain and

---

[66] As Banfield notes, 'Joseph Emonds subdivides the lexicon into an open-class "Dictionary" and a closed-class "Syntacticon" (*Lexicon,* 10). The closed-class members lack highly specified semantic content, having only cognitive syntactic features. Hence the semi-lexical categories are often called (semantically) "light" nouns, verbs, adjectives, and prepositions' (2003, 17).

[67] Beckett uses the expression in *All Strange Away* (Banfield, 2003, 28n68).

the external linguistic scaffolding than 'Joycean' word games, a more super-ficial interference with a system of signifiers, would entail.

At some places, language does seem to take the upper hand and impose its constraints on the text, namely in beautiful instances of alliteration and rhyme produced by the narrator every now and then: 'Dim white and hair so fair that in that dim light dim white' (Beckett, 2009a, 86). That said, the narrator shows little reverence for such cases and would use the beauty of language to thematise it: 'The words too whosesoever. What room for worse! How almost true they sometimes almost ring! How wanting in inanity! Say the night is young alas and take heart. Or better worse say still a watch of night alas to come. A rest of last watch to come. And take heart' (88). The poetic quality of these lines, although most probably invoked for the purposes of parody, is due to the narrator's intelligent use of the affordances language has to offer. What is important to bear in mind is that, although the cognising agent, using its internal computa-tional power, will often mould language according to its expressive needs, language, too, exerts a significant influence as a major constraint on creativity, which generates a robust feedback loop between the neural and external element.

In the narrator's onslaught on language in *Worstward Ho*, the most obvious victims are personal pronouns: except for 'it' and 'they', they are all missing from the text. The battered 'I' finally vanishes from sight, a long overdue realisation of the Unnamable's dream of dispensing with it once and for all. Unlike *Company*, the text in which the 'I' makes only a few furtive appearances and that provided replacements for it by deploying the second-person 'you' and third-person 'he', *Worstward Ho* resorts for the best part of the text to the 'non-pronounial' imperative mood or infinitives.[68] By shifting the focus from the Cartesian 'I' to action and interaction (implied by the imperative mood and its emphasis on verbs), the enactivist nature of the fictional consciousness at work in *Worstward Ho* manifests itself in its most developed form and provides a counterweight to the rich Cartesian imagery that the text undoubtedly still contains.[69]

Worstward Ho is a record of an ongoing cognitive process of creation, a hybrid form of cognition involving a cognitive coupling between the (internal) brain and external elements. Language as an extracranial element is being used to both create the storyworld and evoke the mind of its

---

[68] It seems that Beckett finally managed to implement his intention to escape 'the embarrassment of pronouns' (qtd in Shainberg, 1987, 134; also qtd in Salisbury 2008, 85 with regard to 'what is the word').

[69] A good illustration of the abundance of Cartesian imagery is the astonishing twenty-five times that the word 'skull' appears in this relatively short text.

creator. What is different in these two cases is the representational function of language: while the fictional world the narrator conjures up can still qualify – albeit with difficulty – as representational, the narrator's own fictional mind is not represented in any way at all. In fact, we have absolutely nothing to go on except his use of language – an external structure that amalgamates with the narrator's brain to produce an enactive cognitive system. In other words, the performative element and the imperative mood evoke the mind's energy and dynamism, whereas the broken syntax and ungrammatical sentences may be seen to project its confusion and vulnerability. Here, there is no question of being 'in front of', or engaging in a subject/object relation, as the fictional mind is evoked entirely through an external structure (language) – the same external structure that it uses to create its fictional world from scratch.

Beckett's enactivist evocation of fictional consciousness in *Worstward Ho* chimes in with his own notion of non-relational art as outlined in the Duthuit letter (as discussed earlier). Just like Beckett's, the creative *fictional* mind cannot bear a vacuum and conjures up a world, populating it with humanlike objects – a man, a child, a woman, with detailed references to their body parts and clothes.[70] Thus, a storyworld is reintroduced, albeit in a fragmented and non-linear form: the fleeting, evanescent images being invoked and dismantled in one single breath, the process being repeated time and again. In this autopoietic process of creation, the narrator interacts constantly with the storyworld that is being created, being at the same time the creator of that world and the created entity.[71] Although Cartesian imagery is clearly present in the discourse, the way the discourse is constructed is decidedly anti-Cartesian: there is no pre-given story to tell and no isolated narrating mind representing it as a fixed, stable state of affairs. Instead, the story blends into the discourse and unravels as 'action taken in the moment of speaking' (to paraphrase Porter Abbott's characterisation of Beckett's writing his late prose texts; 1996, x). As an enactive cognitive system, *Worstward Ho* provides a powerful illustration for Beckett's own conviction, expressed in the Duthuit letter, that 'what are called outside and inside are one and the same' (*LSB, II* 140).

---

[70] As Beckett put it in the letter, '[i]f you ask me why the canvas does not stay blank, I can only invoke this unintelligible, unchallengeable need to splash colour on it, even if that means vomiting one's whole being' (*LSB II*, 141). Note the purely physical, organic metaphor of vomit that Beckett uses to express his argument.

[71] This enactive loop bears close similarities to the trope of *Company*'s 'devised deviser devising it all for company'.

'what is the word' (1989)

Beckett's last known work, 'what is the word', is another example in which a cognitive process (in this case, of memory) is enacted in the discourse, although here the narrator finds himself in quite a different predicament. Contrary to the situation in *Worstward Ho*, there is no question here of manipulating or moulding language in a creative way, as the cognising agent is subjected to the sadistic torture of not being able to find the right word. The connection between the internal representation and external referent is severed (possibly by the condition of aphasia),[72] and the victim is desperately trying but unable to restore it. The mutilated muted mind tries to break out of its isolation and back into the world at large, with language being the gateway into that world. The problem is finding the right path by finding the right word. From the 'ultimate cognitive artefact' – an external constraint, but nonetheless a useful and malleable tool – language is transformed into a prison in which the helpless mind is doomed to languish. Of all of Beckett's exasperated and unfortunate narrators, the one in 'what is the word' is probably worst off – he is the only one who is truly isolated and deprived of interaction with the world. Anything – the crutches, the bed, the jar, the mud, the maiming, the violence – seems better than this ultimate, impenetrable confinement within one's own unextended mind. Although the abundance of deixis in the poem ('folly seeing all this – /this – / what is the word – / this this – / this this here – / all this this here – / folly given all this – / seeing – / folly seeing all this this here' and 'there – / over there – / away over there – / afar – / afar away over there – / afaint – / afaint afar away over there what – / what – / what is the word', Beckett, 2009a, 134–4) possibly suggests the existence of some extracranial entity within the storyworld (if one can indeed still speak of a storyworld), the brain is unable to name it, thus precluding any possibility for cognitive interaction and/or extension. In her discussion of this particular passage of the poem, Laura Salisbury notes that '[h]ere, what is left of a perceiving being is thrown amidst a thickened and resistant material world that will not yield to either naming or comprehension, as language becomes a crust of material signifiers that occludes representation' (2008, 82). It seems that in his last piece, Beckett did complete his lifelong artistic quest for the worst, expressed so poignantly in *Worstward Ho* and encoded in its most obvious intertextual reference: 'the worst is not, So long as we can say, "This is the worst"'[73] – the worst is when you *cannot* say it.

---

[72] As is well known, Beckett suffered from temporary aphasia after a fall and loss of consciousness in 1988, and wrote 'what is the word' during his recovery (Van Hulle, 2014a, 209). Van Hulle also suggests that Beckett used this opportunity to investigate how his brain would endure the recovery process, and 'what is the word' can be considered the result of that investigation (208–9).

[73] The reference is obviously to Shakespeare's *King Lear* (Act IV, scene 1).

'what is the word' can also be (and indeed has been) interpreted as an enactment of the cognitive process of artistic creation, in a very material sense. As Van Hulle notes, 'Beckett consciously decided to end his oeuvre with an unfinished work that evokes the workings of a mind, precisely by showing the interaction with the paper during the writing process' (2014a, 208). Perhaps better than any other Beckett text, 'what is the word' represents in a very literal way the nexus between the author's mind and the fictional mind he creates: '[a]gainst the background of the drafts, this text illustrates how Beckett's experience with his manuscripts as part and parcel of the extended mind served as a model to devise a method of evoking the workings of a fictional mind' (208).[74] Even disregarding Beckett's own history as an aphasia patient (the fact that might steer us towards the beguiled biographical approach), the way the narrator gropes in the dark to try and find the right word mirrors Beckett's own search for the right word by means of additions and deletions in the manuscripts. In both cases, it is language, an external cognitive artefact, that guides and obstructs their efforts. Neither endeavour leads to closure, and the right word will not be found: Beckett made a conscious decision to end the text – and by extension his whole oeuvre – in the middle of a sentence (Van Hulle, 2014a, 211).[75] By taking that decision, Beckett 'openly show[ed] his model of the mind as an interactive process: the mind as a constant dialectic of deletions and additions, composition and decomposition' (211).

Conclusion

Labelled a Cartesian from the outset, Beckett was investigated through the prism of mind/world dualism by early Beckett scholarship, which set the tone in Beckett studies for decades to come. Though things have changed in more recent Beckett criticism, the entrenched picture of Beckett the Cartesian endures to this day: for example, in the entry on Beckett in the *Encyclopaedia Britannica*, Descartes is still listed as Beckett's favourite philosopher.[76]

---

[74] It is interesting to note that even in a text that so struggles with its own creation, Beckett apparently manages to smuggle in a subtle intertextual reference, as an homage to Joyce's *Finnegans Wake*, namely its closing line ('Given! A way a lone a last a loved a long the / riverrun, past Eve and Adam's'), in foregrounding the word 'given' and in the following line: 'afaint afar away over there' (Van Hulle 2014a, 211). Thus, Beckett rather symbolically began and ended his writing career by expressing his admiration and respect for Joyce's last work: first by praising its formal properties as 'Work in Progress' (in 'Dante ... Bruno. Vico.. Joyce'), and finally by acknowledging the end of that 'work in progress' (or what had by then become *Finnegans Wake*) by recycling its last sentence in his own last work.

[75] Beckett made a note on the first page of the notebook containing the text of 'Comment dire' that reads 'Keep! for end' (Van Hulle, 2014a, 211).

[76] www.britannica.com/biography/Samuel-Beckett (also mentioned in Feldman, 2006, 30).

As a consequence of this Cartesian bias, the Beckettian fictional mind has come to be perceived as a hermetically sealed container, a 'skullscape', increasingly isolated from its environment as Beckett's oeuvre matures. This representation reflects the traditional cognitivist account of cognition, which treats the mind as a computer-like information-processing device, independent from the lived, phenomenal world it operates in. However, in recent decades a new, postcognitivist paradigm has emerged in philosophy and cognitive science, one that questions the rigid mind/world divide and proposes instead that cognition is not internal but extended, due to the mind's continuous and constitutive interaction with its environment.

The aim of the present study is to use postcognitivist theories of cognition to demonstrate that the lived phenomenal world, although no doubt reduced and fragmented in the later works, nonetheless remained part and parcel of the Beckettian universe. The examples of extended and enactive cognition in Beckett's prose discussed in Section 2 offer a counterweight to the Cartesian bias in early Beckett scholarship sketched in Section 1. In particular, those examples show that instead of being isolated 'skullscapes', Beckett's fictional minds constitute dynamic and hybrid systems that are grounded in the complex and active interplay with the environment they are embedded in, including the cultural and linguistic cognitive scaffolding they continuously rely on. That said, it is important to bear in mind that the reliance of Beckett's fictional minds on external cognitive artefacts (such as rocking chairs, notebooks, or language) does not signify an improvement in their cognitive abilities, which is contrary to what postcognitivist theories postulate. In other words, Beckett's postcognitivist continuum, i.e. the continuous fluctuation between Cartesian dualism, the extended mind theory, and enactivism that the present study suggests, should by no means be seen as a unidirectional progression from worse to better. Instead, it is an oscillation between those poles, pure 'gress' rather than progress, in true Beckettian spirit. Even as part of a hybrid cognitive system, the Beckettian fictional mind is just as lost, confused, and unreliable, fumbling in the dark and trying against all odds to make sense of the world.

Abbreviations

BDMP2 *Samuel Beckett's* L'Innommable / The Unnamable*: a digital genetic edition*, ed. by Dirk Van Hulle, Shane Weller and Vincent Neyt (Brussels: University Press Antwerp, 2013). The Beckett Digital Manuscript Project; module 2, http://www.beckettarchive.org.

BDMP4 *Samuel Beckett's* Molloy*: a digital genetic edition*, ed. by Édouard Magessa O'Reilly, Dirk Van Hulle, Pim Verhulst and Vincent Neyt (Brussels: University Press Antwerp, 2017). The Beckett Digital Manuscript Project; module 4, http://www.beckettarchive.org.

LSB I *The Letters of Samuel Beckett, vol. I, 1929–1940*, ed. by Martha Dow Fehsenfeld and Lois More Overbeck (Cambridge: Cambridge University Press, 2009).

LSB II *The Letters of Samuel Beckett, vol. II, 1941–1956*, ed. by George Craig, Martha Dow Fehsenfeld, Dan Gunn and Lois More Overbeck (Cambridge: Cambridge University Press, 2011).

References

Abbott, H. Porter (1996), *Beckett Writing Beckett: The Author in the Autograph*, Ithaca/London: Cornell University Press.

(2013), *Real Mysteries: Narrative and the Unknowable*, Columbus: The Ohio State University Press.

Admussen, Richard L. (1979), *The Samuel Beckett Manuscripts: A Study*, Boston: G. K. Hall.

Banfield, Ann (2003), 'Beckett's Tattered Syntax', *Representations*, 84:1, pp. 6–29.

Beckett, Samuel (1964), Play: A Play in One Act, in *Play and Two Short Pieces for Radio*. London: Faber and Faber, pp. 9–24.

(1965), *Proust and Three Dialogues with Georges Duthuit*, London: John Calder.

(1984), *Disjecta*, ed. Ruby Cohn, New York: Grove Press.

(1986), *The Complete Dramatic Works*, London: Faber and Faber.

(2009a), *Company, Ill Seen Ill Said, Worstward Ho, Stirrings Still*, ed. Dirk Van Hulle, London: Faber and Faber.

(2009b), *Molloy*, ed. Shane Weller, London: Faber and Faber.

(2009c), *Murphy*, ed. J. C. C. Mays, London: Faber and Faber.

(2009d), *Watt*, ed. C. J. Ackerley, London: Faber and Faber.

(2010a), 'Dante and the Lobster', in *More Pricks Than Kicks*, ed. Cassandra Nelson, London: Faber and Faber, pp. 3–14.

(2010b), *Malone Dies*, ed. Peter Boxall, London: Faber and Faber.

(2010c), *Texts for Nothing and Other Shorter Prose, 1950–1967*, ed. Mark Nixon, London: Faber and Faber.

(2010d), *The Unnamable*, ed. Steven Connor, London: Faber and Faber.

Beloborodova, Olga (2018), *The 'Inward Turn' of Modernism in Samuel Beckett's Work: A Postcognitivist Reassessment*. Unpublished PhD dissertation, University of Antwerp.

Ben-Zvi, Linda (1986), *Samuel Beckett*, Boston: Twaine.

Bernini, Marco (2014), 'Gression, Regression and Beyond: A Cognitive Reading of *The Unnamable*', *Samuel Beckett Today / Aujourd'hui*, 26, pp. 193–210.

Carruthers, Peter (1996), *Language, Thought and Consciousness*. Cambridge: Cambridge University Press.

Chalmers, David J. (1996), *The Conscious Mind: In Search of a Fundamental Theory*, New York: Oxford University Press.

Chatman, Seymour. 1978. *Story and Discourse*, Ithaca: Cornell University Press.

Clark, Andy (1997), *Being There. Putting Brain, Body, and World Together Again*, Cambridge, MA: The MIT Press.

Clark, Andy and David Chalmers [1998] (2010), 'The Extended Mind', in Richard Menary (ed.), *The Extended Mind*, Cambridge, MA: The MIT Press, pp. 27–42.

Cohn, Ruby (1962), *Samuel Beckett: The Comic Gamut*, New Brunswick: Rutgers University Press.

(1965), 'Philosophical Fragments in the Works of Samuel Beckett', in Martin Esslin (ed.), *Samuel Beckett: A Collection of Critical Essays*, Englewood Cliffs: Prentice-Hall, pp. 169–177.

(1980), *Just Play*, Princeton: Princeton University Press.

Cohn, Ruby, Mona Van Duyn, Jarvis Thurston, and Carl Hartman (eds.) (1959), *Perspective: A Quarterly of Literature and the Arts*, 11:3.

Craig, George Martha Dow Fehsenfeld, Dan Gunn, and Lois More Overbeck (2011), *The Letters of Samuel Beckett, vol. II, 1941–1956*, Cambridge: Cambridge University Press.

Dennett, Daniel (1993), *Consciousness Explained*, London: Penguin.

Di Paolo, Ezequiel A., Marieke Rohde, and Hanne De Jaegher (2010), 'Horizons for the Enactive Mind: Values, Social Interaction, and Play', in John Stewart, Olivier Gapenne, and Ezequiel A. Di Paolo (eds), *Enaction: Toward a New Paradigm for Cognitive Science*, Cambridge, MA: MIT Press, pp. 33–87.

Dow Fehsenfeld, Martha and Lois More Overbeck (eds) (2009), *The Letters of Samuel Beckett, vol. I, 1929–1940*, Cambridge: Cambridge University Press.

Esslin, Martin (ed.) (1965), *Samuel Beckett: A Collection of Critical Essays*, Englewood Cliffs: Prentice-Hall.

(1986), 'Samuel Beckett and the Art of Radio', in S. E. Gontarski (ed.), *On Beckett: Essays and Criticism*, New York: Grove Press, pp. 360–84.

Feldman, Matthew (2006), *Beckett's Books: A Cultural History of Samuel Beckett's 'Interwar' Notes*, New York/London: Continuum.

Feldman, Matthew, and Karim Mamdani (eds.) (2015), *Beckett / Philosophy*, Stuttgart: Ibidem Verlag.

Fifield, Peter (2015), '"Of being – and remaining": Beckett's Early Greek Philosophy', in Matthew Feldman and Karim Mamdani (eds.), *Beckett / Philosophy*, Stuttgart: Ibidem Verlag, pp. 127–50.

Fletcher, John (1964), *The Novels of Samuel Beckett*, London: Chatto and Windus.

Fletcher, John and John Spurling (1972), *Beckett. A Study of his Plays*, London: Methuen.

Gauker, Christopher (1990), 'How to learn a language like a chimpanzee', *Philosophical Psychology*, 3:1, pp. 31–53.

Gontarski, S. E. (1985), *The Intent of Undoing in Samuel Beckett's Dramatic Texts*, Bloomington: Indiana University Press.

Hamilton, Alice, and Kenneth Hamilton (1976), 'The Guffaw of the Abderite: Samuel Beckett's Use of Democritus', *Mosaic: An Interdisciplinary Critical Journal*, 9:2, pp. 1–13.

Herman, David (2011), 'Re-minding Modernism', in David Herman, (ed.), *The Emergence of Mind. Representations of Consciousness in Narrative Discourse in English*, Lincoln: University of Nebraska Press, pp. 243–72.

Hesla, David (1971), *The Shape of Chaos: An Interpretation of the Art of Samuel Beckett*, Minneapolis: University of Minnesota Press.

Hutto, Daniel D. and Erik Myin (2013), *Radicalizing Enactivism. Basic Minds without Content*, Cambridge, MA: The MIT Press.

James, William [1904] (1996), 'Does "Consciousness" Exist?', in Eugene Taylor and Robert Wozniak (eds.), *Pure Experience. The Responses to William James*, Bristol: Thoemmes Press, pp. 1–17.

Katz, Daniel (1999), *'Saying I no more': Subjectivity and Consciousness in the Prose of Samuel Beckett*, Evanston: Northwestern University Press.

Kenner, Hugh (1961), *Samuel Beckett: A Critical Study*, Berkeley: University of California Press.

Knowlson, James (1996), *Damned to Fame. The Life of Samuel Beckett*, London: Bloomsbury.

Kroll, Jeri (1977), 'The Surd as Inadmissible Evidence: The Case of Attorney General v. Henry McCabe', *Journal of Beckett Studies*, 2, pp. 47–58.

Lane, Richard (ed.) (2002), *Beckett and Philosophy*, London: Palgrave.

Maude, Ulrika (2009), *Beckett, Technology and the Body*, Cambridge: Cambridge University Press.

Menary, Richard (2007), 'Writing as Thinking', *Language Sciences*, 29:5, pp. 621–32.

Merleau-Ponty, Maurice [1945] (1962), *Phenomenology of Perception*, trans. Colin Smith, London: Routledge.

Mintz, Samuel (1959), 'Beckett's *Murphy*: A Cartesian Novel', *Perspective: A Quarterly of Literature and the Arts*, 11:3, pp. 156–65.

Mooney, Michael E. (1982), 'Presocratic Scepticism: Samuel Beckett's *Murphy* Reconsidered', *ELH [English Literary History]*, 49:1, pp. 214–34.

Moran, Dermot (2006), 'Beckett and Philosophy', in Christopher Murray (ed.), *Samuel Beckett: 100 Years: Centenary Essays*, Dublin: New Island Publishers, pp. 93–109.

Morot-Sir, Edouard (1976), 'Samuel Beckett and Cartesian Emblems', in Edouard Morot-Sir, Howard Harper, and Dougald McMillan III (eds.), *Samuel Beckett and the Art of Rhetoric*, Chapel Hill: University of North Carolina Department of Romance Languages, pp. 25–104.

Norman, Donald (1993), *Things that Make Us Smart: Defending Human Attributes in the Age of the Machine*, Boston: Addison-Wesley.

O'Reilly, Édouard Magessa, Dirk Van Hulle, and Pim Verhulst (2017), *The Making of Samuel Beckett's 'Molloy'*, Brussels and London: University Press Antwerp and Bloomsbury.

Pattie, David (2000), *Samuel Beckett*, London/New York: Routledge.

Pilling, John (1999), *Beckett's 'Dream' Notebook*, Reading: Beckett International Foundation.

(2011), *Samuel Beckett's 'More Pricks Than Kicks': In A Strait Of Two Wills*, London: Bloomsbury.

Pothast, Ulrich (2008), *The Metaphysical Vision: Arthur Schopenhauer's Philosophy of Art and Life and Samuel Beckett's Own Way to Make Use of It*, New York: Peter Lang.

Pountney, Rosemary (1988), *Theatre of Shadows: Samuel Beckett's Drama 1956–1976*, Gerrards Cross: Colin Smythe.

Rodaway, Paul (1994), *Sensuous Geographies: Body, Sense, and Place*, London: Routledge.

Rowlands, Mark (2010), *The New Science of the Mind*, Cambridge, MA: The MIT Press.

(2015), 'Consciousness Unbound', *Journal of Consciousness Studies*, 22:3–4, pp. 34–51.

Ryle, Gilbert [1949] (2000), *The Concept of Mind*, London: Penguin.

Salisbury, Laura (2008), '"What Is the Word": Beckett's Aphasic Modernism', *Journal of Beckett Studies*, 17: 1–2, pp. 78–126.

Scruton, Roger (1983), 'Beckett and the Cartesian Soul', in *The Aesthetic Understanding: Essays in the Philosophy of Art and Culture*, London/New York: Methuen, pp. 222–41.

Shainberg, Lawrence (1987), 'Exorcising Beckett', *The Paris Review*, 29:104, pp. 100–36.

Sheehan, Paul (2017), 'Scenes of Writing: Beckett and the Technology of Inscription', *Samuel Beckett Today / Aujourd'hui*, 29:1, pp. 138–49.

Stewart, John (2010), 'Foundational Issues in Enaction as a Paradigm for Cognitive Science', in John Stewart, Olivier Gapenne, and Ezequiel

A. Di Paolo (eds.), *Enaction: Toward a New Paradigm for Cognitive Science*, Cambridge, MA: MIT Press, pp. 1–31.

Tajiri, Yoshiki (2007), *Samuel Beckett and the Prosthetic Body*, London: Palgrave Macmillan.

Tucker, David (2012), *Samuel Beckett and Arnold Geulincx*, London: Bloomsbury.

Van Hulle, Dirk (2012), 'The Extended Mind and Multiple Drafts: Beckett's Models of the Mind and the Postcognitivist Paradigm', *Samuel Beckett Today / Aujourd'hui*, 24:1, pp. 277–90.

(2014a), *Modern Manuscripts. The Extended Mind and Creative Undoing from Darwin to Beckett and Beyond*, London: Bloomsbury.

(2014b), 'The Obidil and the Man of Glass', *Samuel Beckett Today / Aujourd'hui*, 26:1, pp. 25–39.

(2018), 'Authors' Libraries and the Extended Mind: The Case of Joyce's Books', in Sylvain Belluc and Valerie Benejam (eds.), *Cognitive Joyce*, London: Palgrave Macmillan, pp. 65–82.

Van Hulle, Dirk, and Mark Nixon (2013), *Samuel Beckett's Library*, Cambridge: Cambridge University Press.

Van Hulle, Dirk, and Pim Verhulst (2017), *The Making of Samuel Beckett's 'Malone meurt'/'Malone Dies'*, Brussels and London: University Press Antwerp and Bloomsbury.

Van Hulle, Dirk, and Shane Weller (2014), *The Making of Samuel Beckett's 'L'Innommable'/'The Unnamable'*, Brussels and London: University Press Antwerp and Bloomsbury.

Varela, Francisco J., Evan Thompson, and Eleonor Rosch (1991), *The Embodied Mind: Cognitive Science and Human Experience*, Cambridge, MA: The MIT Press.

Weller, Shane (2018), 'From Language Revolution to Literature of the Unword: Beckett as Late Modernist', in Olga Beloborodova, Dirk Van Hulle, and Pim Verhulst (eds.), *Beckett and Modernism*, London: Palgrave Macmillan, pp. 37–52.

Woolf, Virginia [1917] (2000), 'The Mark on the Wall', in *Selected Short Stories*, London: Penguin Modern Classics.

Worth, Katherine (1981), 'Beckett and the Radio Medium', in John Drakakis (ed.), *British Radio Drama*, Cambridge: Cambridge University Press, pp. 191–217.

Zilliacus, Clas (1976), *Beckett and Broadcasting: A Study of the Works of Samuel Beckett for and in Radio and Television*, Åbo: Åbo Akademi.

Cambridge Elements ≡

Beckett Studies

Dirk Van Hulle

University of Oxford

Dirk Van Hulle is Professor of Bibliography and Modern Book History at the University of Oxford and director of the Centre for Manuscript Genetics at the University of Antwerp.

Mark Nixon

University of Reading

Mark Nixon is Associate Professor in Modern Literature at the University of Reading and the Co-Director of the Beckett International Foundation.

About the Series

This series presents cutting-edge research by distinguished and emerging scholars, providing space for the most relevant debates informing Beckett studies as well as neglected aspects of his work. In times of technological development, religious radicalism, unprecedented migration, gender fluidity, environmental and social crisis, Beckett's works find increased resonance. Elements in Beckett Studies is a key resource for readers interested in the current state of the field.

Cambridge Elements ☰

Beckett Studies

Elements in the Series

Experimental Beckett: Contemporary Performance Practices
Nicholas E. Johnson and Jonathan Heron

Postcognitivist Beckett
Olga Beloborodova

A full series listing is available at: www.cambridge.org/eibs

Printed in the United States
By Bookmasters